UP THE I.V. POLE

A Financial Manual for Nurses

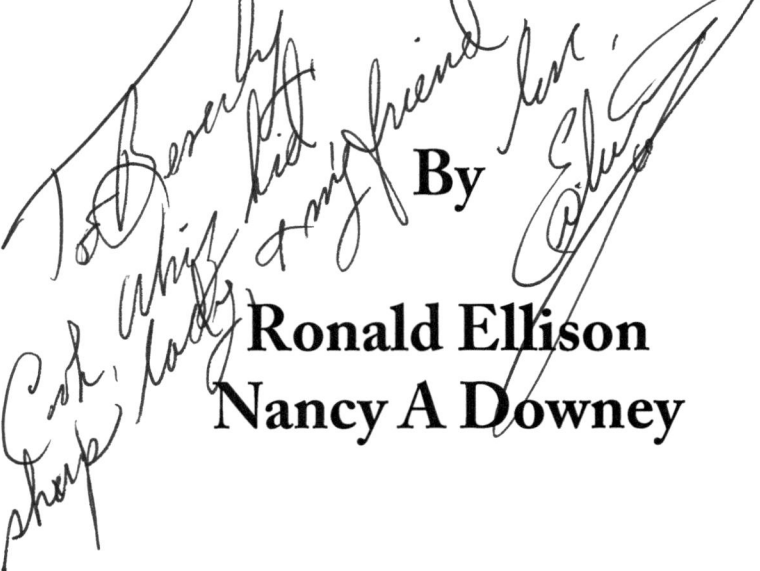

By

Ronald Ellison
Nancy A Downey

authorHOUSE™

1663 LIBERTY DRIVE, SUITE 200
BLOOMINGTON, INDIANA 47403
(800) 839-8640
WWW.AUTHORHOUSE.COM

AuthorHouse™
1663 Liberty Drive, Suite 200
Bloomington, IN 47403
www.authorhouse.com
Phone: 1-800-839-8640

AuthorHouse™ *UK Ltd.*
500 Avebury Boulevard
Central Milton Keynes, MK9 2BE
www.authorhouse.co.uk
Phone: 08001974150

First published by AuthorHouse   4/4/2007

ISBN: 978-1-4208-8099-1 (sc)

Printed in the United States of America
Bloomington, Indiana

This book is printed on acid-free paper.

TABLE OF CONTENTS

PROLOGUE

George Orwell said that writing a book (er, manual) is a "long, exhausting struggle, like a long bout of some painful illness." It was Orwell's conclusion that one would never undertake such a task if not driven by "some demon one can neither resist nor understand." For us there were three demons: informative, entertaining and thought provoking. To try to unravel a few of the mysteries and myths of an important but imposing subject for a specialized audience in an informative, entertaining and thought-provoking way, now that's a prescription for the tranquilizer of your choice.

At first we considered the tip-toeing-through-the-tulips approach, a format much in vogue today with the PC crowd. But much truer to our style and liking is what we finally decided on, the old sink-or-swim technique. For the first few minutes the water's bound to be cold. Like many things in life, however, it's the after glow you leave with that's paramount.

A few years ago a friend retired after spending nearly 25 years in medicine. He decided to seek a second career, hardly a novel event in today's world, this time in sales. Though he had never sold any official products in his life, after filling out gobs of forms and sitting through several interviews, our friend weeks later found himself one sunny, bright Southern California morning on the 15th floor of a modern high rise, sitting in an office festooned with enough sales awards and commemorative plaques to make a Heisman Trophy winner envious. A man in his early 50s, slightly white around the temples, wearing the obligatory corporate uniform, blue suit, plain white shirt and plain red tie sat facing him. The general manager and vice president of sales studied our friend's application folder for several minutes before looking up.

"I don't see anything here," the general manager said, breaking the long silence, "that says you have any sales experience. What makes you think you can sell our product?"

Clearing his throat after what seemed a full 45 seconds of silence, our friend replied:

"Because for the last 25 years or so I have been selling what is the toughest product on the planet to sell."

A perplexed look thick enough to cut with a chain saw suddenly captured the general manager's face. It was as if you could see the wheels of his gray matter kicking up debris. "What could possibly be more difficult to sell than a high-ticket product like ours?" the look seemed to be asking. "Even our top sales people manage to sell only a handful a year."

"And just what is that?" the sales manager finally probed.

"Getting people to change their behavior," our friend responded. "That's the most difficult sell on earth."

So we're open to whatever criticism may come if in writing this manual it proves thought provoking, informative and entertaining. And should it by some quirk of luck alter the behavior of just one person (investor), nurse and put her or him on the path to achieving her or his goals, the time and energy and effort will have been like a Midwestern picnic to a horde of mosquitoes on a warm summer evening, a mighty, loveable feast.

In writing a book (er, manual) there are always too many people to thank. So we will doubtless leave someone of importance out, like some of the now faceless students over the years we bounced many of these ideas off. As the saying goes, it's always easier to get forgiveness than permission. So forgive us if we've omitted anyone.

Thanks to Michelle Smith who did most of the charts and helped with the proof reading. Michelle is a computer whiz of the first magnitude. She is easy to work with and has the patience of half a dozen saints. Thanks also to Eileen Fischer of Las Vegas, a true artist by any definition one would choose to define it. She did all the cartoons and if she ever had any doubts about the undertaking, never let them show. Thanks to Tiffany Mendoza-Samoff for her hours of reviewing the manual and good coffee making. Thanks to Ken Blasingham, one of the founders of Blasingham and Ellison Financial Group in Newport Beach, California. If there's a more laid-back guy to work with, we have yet to cross his trail.

A special thanks to Ronal Q. Ellison, the best daughter a father ever had, for her support and encouragement, not to mention the many rousing debates over the years. Though tiny in stature, she always gave as good, if not then some, as she received. She is in her own right a leather-tough, consummate professional in the rough and wooly world of electronic media. For this reason it should be noted that any opinions expressed here completely and entirely reflect those of Papa Ellison and Ms. Nancy Downey and no one else. And a big thanks to Margaret A. Leonard-Downey, the best daughter a mother ever had. Though professionally trained to cut and dye a mean head of hair, for reasons of her own she decided to follow her mother's professional footsteps. She is a nurse. And finally, special thanks to Molly Downey. You are missed, but never forgotten.

Who would have thought it, a manual about investing for nurses? Sounds like a novel idea. You bet it does. When I first proposed the idea to a publisher, in fact, several publishers, invariably the initial response was: "Why nurses?" Well, there are probably a hundred good answers, starting with the one my co-author gave me. His mother was a nurse and so am I. As it turned out, his dad died when he was 10 years old, leaving his mother to support the entire family with her nursing degree. And irrespective of what you may think about whether nurses are paid poorly or fairly today, back then nurses' pay rivaled a bad case of pernicious anemia. And social issues like female equality and equal pay were so far on the back burner that you couldn't find the stove. Back then was light years from April 2003 when in its 186-year history the first woman was named dean of Harvard's law school. And back then was an eon from today when a divorced or widowed woman could not get credit in her own name.

He recalled how his mother knew little to nothing about finances and whatever she earned went to keep the family afloat.(Incidentally, dealing with publishers is a lot like trying to start IVs on statues. If you're into self-flagellation I highly recommend it. It's right up there with marrying an alcoholic or volunteering weekly for a sigmoidoscopy.) One has to learn to forgive publishers their ignorance. I have. As for answers, how about: "Nurses are people too." Bookstores are rife with books for "dummies." Nearly everything from how to potty train your pet aardvark to gardening for gnomes to repairing the diesel engine on your favorite granddad Lester's old Sherman tank has been done, how about a good book (sorry, manual) for thousands of non-dummies?" In my own case my husband, who served two combat tours of duty with the airborne in Vietnam, suffering only minor injuries, keeled over from a myocardial infarction and died at age 50, leaving two children, me and a large mortgage payment behind.

In my own career I have worked in nursing from geriatrics to gastroenterology to urology to neurosurgery to clinical research and public health. As an NP, I practiced in-patient and outpatient medicine. At one point, not my proudest moment or the best decision of my life, I left a secure staff position to join a start-up oncology research firm. Great promise and riches lay just ahead. A brief year and a half later, however, the company downsized and I found myself jobless and with a drawer full of essentially worthless stock certificates. Nearly 15 years later, my former employer, barely a shell of its old self, is still there and so are the stock certificates. I am not sure what the net worth of my old employer is, but for a few bucks and the stock certificates I am sure you can still purchase a hot cup of green tea. To say it was a wake-up call is to acknowledge that diabetics can develop foot ulcers.

The statistics say women, though the gap is narrowing, live longer than men. That means a lot of nurses might find themselves surviving not one but two spouses. (Ok, we know that there are a lot of male nurses out there doing a great job, so don't get upset. We're not discriminating. These are just the statistics!) The numbers also say, according to a 2000

U.S. Census Bureau study, that 91 percent of registered nurses are female, but their median income is $42,000, $3,000 less than male RNs. The census report tracked 1999 income data for 505 different job categories and the study is based on a subset of 400 job categories with at least 10,000 year-round, full-time workers each with at least 1,000 male and 1,000 female workers. It concluded women on average earn 74 cents to the one dollar men earned. That means unless things change, or you hit the lottery, most of you will be planning your investments and retirement with roughly 25 percent less than most males. Where is that written in the genetic code of equal opportunity and the pursuit of life, liberty and your soul mate?

Perhaps the best answer is nurses are decision makers; they make lots and lots of decisions everyday, some of them quite important decisions. And investing, like life, is about a series of decisions. So here's a decision for you: You must decide if you want to read this book (sorry, manual!). Prejudice and all that other stuff aside, I think you'll enjoy the read. I guarantee you'll learn something.

Nancy A. Downey, BSRN, MSRN, NP

The Department of Health and Human Services' Health Resources and Service Administration conducted the survey, which gathered information from nurses every four years. These results were released in late December 2005. Please look at the charts below:

CHAPTER ONE

Even if you're on the right track, if you just sit there you'll still get run over.

Will Rogers

CREATIVITY AND CREDIT

It may seem strange to begin a manual about investing for nurses with a chapter on creativity. Don't panic! You're on the right track, but don't just sit there. Keep turning those pages. Creativity can come from many sources. But in the corporate or financial world it usually begins with: "How can we sell more products?" Now don't get flustered or confused. Product isn't always a good, like refrigerators or cars (we'll get to them later). Product can be a service, like carpet cleaning or hair styling or, for that matter, health care.

Several years ago when the late Princess Diana had just become Lady Diana, she sported a certain hairstyle. In fact, it was near impossible to visit London at the time and not see some young (and more than a few older) women jaunting about with a similar coiffure. You might say Princess Diana was good for business. In many ways, she became a product. And even in death, she still is. And for that matter, so is Elvis.

When it comes to creativity artists, architects, poets, sculptors, writers, movie directors and musicians, or anyone else you consider to be among the creative set, have nothing on all those corporate finance officers, bankers and the myriad minions of Wall Street. In fact, God may not have anything on these financial folks. But back to the big question: How can we sell more products? If the word credit comes to mind, you're starting to get it.

Unless you've been living on another planet (and some of us have, think politicians with presidential aspirations!) the last few years, you realize that traffic is a major problem in most major American cities. Here in Southern California where I live, people have a euphemism for heavy-duty, profanity-producing traffic, congestion. That's right; they call it congestion with a big C. Radio announcers and bureaucrats love the term. Lungs get congested. Freeways get clogged. So how did all those cars get there? No, Immaculate Conception is incorrect. But that's close. For the answer (and the solution to all that congestion) we have to take a brief detour back through the pages of time to yesteryear and our old buddy American humorist Will Rogers.

"The only way to solve the traffic problems of the country," Rogers pointed out more than 70 years ago in what today is hardly a laughing matter, "is to pass a law that only paid-for cars are allowed to use the highways."

What Rogers was really talking about, whether he realized it we will never know, is the downside of credit. Yes, you're reading this correctly; we did say CREDIT. In the United States about one out of every other American owns an automobile. Now we all know some own more than one, but with a population of nearly 300 million that's roughly about 150 million cars. China, on the other hand, a huge country that is rapidly undergoing Western-style industrialization, sports a population of a 1.3 billion. Just imagine if every second Chinese owned a car— again the U.S. average; that would one day put 600 million cars in China alone. The current world total of cars is 540 million, so you're starting to get the picture. While you're at it, imagine the infrastructure from parking lots to highways to gas stations that China would need to support all those cars, not to mention the traffic cops.

And that brings us back to credit. Despite what biblical scholars tell us, just suppose God never took that seventh day off. Painful as it may be to contemplate, just suppose He was busy creating the concept of credit. Remember all those corporate finance officers, bankers and Wall Street minions came from somewhere. We could blame Harvard, but Harvard's too busy dealing with the issues of grade inflation and free speech.

Credit can be good with its good side. And credit can be bad. Credit allows us to trade-in those tattered-pogo sticks and cruise around righteously perched above it all in those shiny new SUVs for the next three or four years and then, presto, repeat the whole thing. In fact, as one business associate recently put it, trying to take all those SUVs from all those soccer moms who seem to believe that owning an SUV is their constitutional God-given right would be tougher than trying to pry lose their first born at birth.

Now how many Americans do you think either own or are buying their homes, most of them on credit? Imagine if we all got up one morning and decided to drive our houses to work. Now that would create some congestion. Don't laugh. Someone has already thought of it. I don't know about you, but I've been stuck behind my share of Good Neighbor Sams in morning rush hour congestion. I don't want to get too clinical here, but for years I had a couple of guys, retirees, who used to show up randomly for their clinic appointments who sold their homes when they retired and bought those gargantuan abortions on wheels.

Years ago the late Dinah Shore (for you younger folks, Dinah was a pop singer) had a television show sponsored by Chevrolet. At the opening and closing of the show each week, Dinah would belt out: "See the USA in your Chevrolet. America is asking you to call." Those were the pre-Toyota days and it was a time not too long after President Eisenhower laid the groundwork for the nation's interstate highway system that eventually made anachronisms of such standard thoroughfares as Route 66. In many ways the interstate highway system was the precursor of the Internet: one connects the nation, the other the world. It was a call to promote travel. And soon folks were getting their kicks on the gleaming new ribbons of interstates instead of old Route 66. Well, my clinic guys were seeing the land of the Stars and Stripes in their houses. And, in most cases, thanks to credit, so are a lot of other folks.

The point here is creativity is a lot like yin and yang. If you see yin bopping down the pike, you can bet yang is not far behind. It took creativity to create credit. And once created it's pretty difficult to get the credit genie back in the old bottle. So the first step to getting a handle on understanding investing is to get a handle on credit and how and why it was created and how and why it can help or hurt you. Besides, the topic of credit will come again when we get to bonds. To be forewarned, as they say, is to prevent them from coming back and biting you where you'd least like to be chomped, the pocketbook.

Here in Southern California, the land of the automobile, vanity plates and recall elections, it isn't uncommon to see some guy or gal slogging along the freeway in the morning with a bumper sticker that reads: "I owe, I owe. Off to work I go." That's credit. Some may mistake it for humor, but it's really credit. So unless you come to an understanding of credit and how and why it can be your best friend or your worst enemy and get a grip on it, you'll probably never realize your dream of early or secure retirement or both.

The U.S. has about an $11 trillion economy or GDP. Keep this chart in mind as you proceed through the chapter. In 2003 personal consumption was nearly 72 % of GDP. To put it in simple terms that's a big number. And note the trend. So here's a question to contemplate: what do you think might happen if one fine day consumers decided to suddenly pack it in? You don't know it yet, but later you will see that much of this increase in personal consumption parallels the decline in interest rates and the rise in stock market valuations since 1982. Some economists refer to this phenomenon as the "wealth effect." In reality, and this is getting a bit ahead of the story, there have been two wealth effects—one in equities or stocks, the other in real estate.

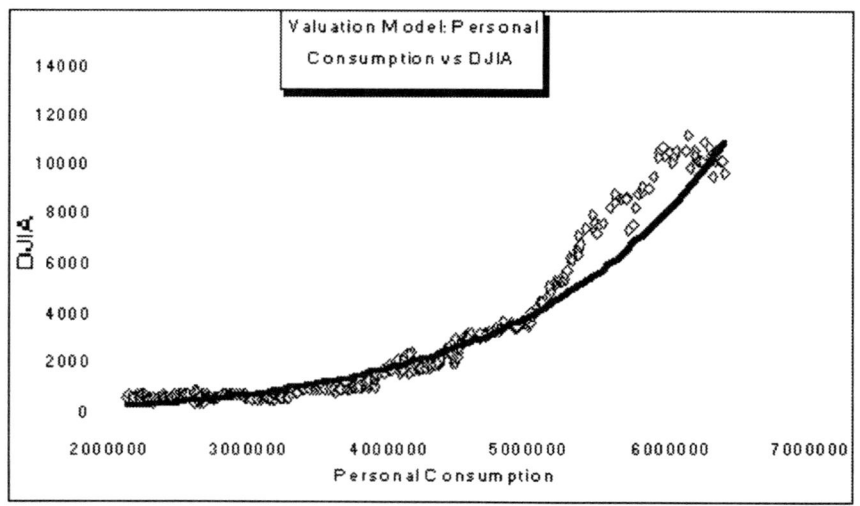

Notice as the Dow Jones Industrial average increased in value personal Consumption sky rocketed. This is what economists refer to as the "Wealth Effect".

Some people would deny that that there are good folks and bad folks in the world. In a semi-free nation such as ours that's their prerogative. But there is no denying that when it comes to credit, there is definitely good credit and bad credit. And at the risk of getting a bit technical, something any nurse worth her or his RN pin should grasp, we'll explain the difference just in case you may not know. To do so, however, will require a brief excursion into a land were many folks (not just nurses) often fear to tread—the Land of Economics.

We realize that for many it is a dreary dismal place, but that's not really why it's often referred to as the Dismal Science. Philosophers and social engineers are fond of citing that we are all human beings. Well, the bottom line is, like it or otherwise, we are all economic beings too; and most of us have finite resources. Try to keep that fact in mind along the journey. And if you have any difficulty, just think about all those Green weenies and environmental terrorists on the environmental front. Most believe they coined the phrase.

So what's the difference between good debt and bad debt? In and of itself debt is not bad. In our ultra-modern world, as one writer has put it, debt "embodies the symbiosis of the three progressive classes of people in the economy: savers, producers and inventors." Here we would substitute the term entrepreneurs for inventors, but the point is the same. "Debt is the instrument whereby savers," he continues, "can exchange wealth for income. Debt is the instrument whereby producers can avail themselves of the best technology in order to produce the highest output per input of labor and capital, for the benefit of everybody. Debt is the instrument whereby inventors [entrepreneurs] can exchange their future wealth for present income to support research and development."

Sounds all rather complicated, but hang on. We warned you the water would be brisk at first.

We're not quite finished. "Debt makes it possible to extend the division of labor between contemporaries to the division of labor between generations removed from one another in time. Debt makes the emancipation of savings possible." Stop and think about this for a second. You ask someone, a friend, for a loan. That person, at least as far as you believe, must have the money somewhere, in a checking account or savings account, a coffee can or even in his or her wallet. If you don't have any savings how could you lend anyone any money, assuming you chose to? The answer is you can't. So debt makes the emancipation of savings possible.

In order to borrow money, and that's what you're doing whether you actually get the cash in hand or purchase a television set, and take on debt, someone must have the money saved up to lend to you. In many cases it is a bank, a merchant or a credit card company. And in most cases the bank usually owns the credit card company. It is similar to what economists call vertical integration. To economists vertical integration is when you own the mine that produces the raw material, and you own the factory that uses the raw material to make the product and you own the transportation company that owns the trucks you use to ship the finished product to your customer.

Now let's break this down. You buy a car on time or credit. You just entered into a contract. The definition of a contract is both sides must receive, or there must be, consideration. What's the consideration?

You get the car now and the lender gets the promise of future income or future wealth in exchange. No consideration, no contract. Pretty simple stuff, you must admit. So debt becomes the catalyst, you could say, for the creation of future income and wealth. It's that basic. "In other words," to quote our previous author, "through the agency of debt, present wealth and present income will find their socially most beneficial, optimal applications." You need reliable transportation to get to work everyday, the lender seeks future income and wealth in exchange. Some folks call it creative financing. We told you early on about that term creativity.

I have a car or a whole lot full of cars I don't need. I created that car or those cars with my savings. You don't have the money to pay cash for one. So my savings makes the creation of your debt possible. And your debt emancipates my savings, in most cases guaranteeing me more future income than my savings alone would produce. You get what you need and I forego the present for the creation of future wealth and income. Is that any different from a friend who says: "Just pay me back when you get it? I don't need the cash right now?" The difference is if he or she is a true friend, he doesn't charge you any carrying costs or interest. In medical terms it could be called circulation. Those cars are just sitting there on my lot; you're just sitting there without a reliable way to get to your employment. You have a need and so do I. Call it a lack of liquidity or circulation or whatever you want. The need exists.

Just for the heck of it, say the automobile dealer you purchased the car from dies and his son takes over the business. Do you still have to pay back the loan? Yes. Did the debt brook a generation? Yes. So what's the point, you ask? Just this: debt, as most everyone knows, is not without its perils. Like many things in life, if not properly handled it can be dangerous. Think here about Petri dishes and mad scientists. Bad debt can become epidemic. Most things in life have a critical mass, including you and me. So that brings us to an important distinction, the difference between good and bad debt, what this chapter is really all about.

Oh yes, there is one, and it's hardly subjective. And here it is. The importance of debt is related to its marginal productivity. Buying that car so you can get to work and earn a living allowed you to be productive. Say, however, you already owned five cars, yet you took on debt to buy another one. Well, you can only drive one to work everyday, so five of those cars, whether you like them and just want them or whatever, add zilch to your overall productivity. It is what 19th Century sociologist Thorstein Veblen called "conspicuous consumption." And that's the distinction between good and bad debt. Does it add to your productivity? Does that 30th pair of new shoes you just purchased on credit and tossed into your closet add to your productivity? Now don't get into a politically-correct twit here. Even if you bought half of those shoes for work, how many can you wear at once? And it's highly unlikely even the most attentive will notice the last time you wore those cobalt blue pumps to the job.

In formal terms it has to do with a ratio, the ratio of the net increase in Gross Domestic Product (GDP) to the increase in debt. Now don't get in a twitter here, either. Gross domestic product is the total output of a sovereign country or state. California is a sovereign state within a sovereign country, the United States of America, with an output that makes it the sixth largest GDP or economy in the world. The largest, you guessed it, the good ole USA with a GDP of about $11 trillion a year. That's not chump change.

Like any ratio, the ratio between the net increase in GDP to the increase in debt reveals something vitally important. Think, for instance, about the ratio of carbohydrate intake to blood sugar levels in diabetics. Or for that matter the ratio between insulin dosage to carbohydrate intake and exercise. What, for example, is the ratio in diabetic patients between the number of calories consumed and their blood sugars? Or, to twist it just slightly, all other things equal, how about the ratio between patients who have smoked cigarettes for 25 years and their possibilities of developing cardiovascular disease? Ratios are not perfect, but they matter. Debt, like that new car you just purchased to get to work, has to be serviced. And the ratio we're talking about here shows whether the debt can be serviced or amortized (paid for) out of income or whether new debt will have to be incurred for that purpose. Think again about that diabetic. Will you have to increase his insulin dose or other medication to control his blood sugar? In other words, can the diabetic patient control his blood sugar with diet and his current insulin dose or will you have to have him increase his dose?

Everybody probably has either heard of or knows of someone who pays off one credit card by opening up another credit card. In short, income or cash flow is inadequate to service the debt, hardly a good thing whether you're talking about individuals, corporations or countries. And if you're talking countries think Argentina or America. So now you have it: good debt, whether its countries, corporations or people, is seen as debt that allows one to become more productive, gain employment, grow a business, produce a better product, capture more market share, deliver better service or care; you fill in the blanks. With the exception of a feel-good factor and an increased service burden, bad debt adds nothing you really desire to the equation. And here's the real hang-up, once the marginal productivity of debt is permitted to significantly decline, or worse case scenario, become negative, the point of critical mass is reached and the whole mess becomes uncontrollable. Next stop: destruction.

Only two ways to destroy debt exists. You can default or try to inflate your way out of it. Folks like you and me usually default because we don't have the luxury, as governments do, of inflating our way free. Though you could argue that taking on that second or third job to help control the debt is similar to inflating one's way out of it. The big difference here, however, is there are only 24 hours in one day and the number of jobs one can work is limited. On the other hand, there is no limit to a government's ability to inflate its way out of debt. Because of deflation during the Great Depression in the 1930s lots of folks defaulted. During the Vietnam era our government sought to inflate its way clear. You remember LBJ, the Great Society and the war in Southeast Asia that our wonderful president privately believed we couldn't win but still sent young, unsuspecting Americans by the thousands there to die? That was the period of the welfare-warfare state more informally known as guns and butter. So a basic definition is inflation represents a rapid increase in the money supply, deflation a rapid decrease in the money supply with prices adjusting accordingly over time.

It's a debatable point, however, which of the two is the least socially desirable, inflation or deflation. Inflation plays havoc with your purchasing power. True deflation dries up liquidity and makes paying back debts more onerous. Inflation favors the debtor;

deflation the creditor. At least that's what most of today's economists believe; the truth is true deflation is good for the consumer because his purchasing power is increasing daily, but what's that old saying about never disturb a sleeping economist? And here's a little investment side note to log away. During the last period in the U.S. of real deflation, 1929 to 1932, the only two investments that did well were gold and bonds. That's pretty unusual. To have the price of gold and the price of bonds appreciating at the same time is akin to saying that wet and dry mean the same thing. What you need to know and understand is this: One man's pork is another man's poison. And it has always been such. To put it another way, one man's debt is another man's asset. How many times have you heard about someone who had to sell a house, a car or whatever?

Billionaire Sam Zell, the Chicago real estate magnet, is to real estate what Bill Gross is to bonds. His nickname is the Grave Dancer. Zell likes to buy properties when they have one foot in Intensive Care and the other on life support. Zell's zealousness for cheap properties is nothing more than a simple fulfillment of the supply-demand curves economists love to talk about. If supply is plentiful and demand diminished, prices are most likely going to be cheap.

Armed with such information buyers will hardly ever pay the asking price or the true market value. So here is the rub. Wealth can be destroyed either by inflation or by deflation and both are anti-social and without any redeeming qualities. So say the so-called experts. Both can be prevented, however, by sound economic policy and observing the marginal productivity of debt. You could say: if you don't need it, don't buy it. Now that's not a formula that will hardly please your elected officials, since consumption equals about two-third of the U.S. economy and many politicians after 911 tried to sell the idea that consuming was patriotic. But you can bet on one thing: if the marginal productivity of your debt becomes negative, don't expect any knocks on your door any time soon from these folks to help bail you out.

Unless you have friends in high places, and most of us don't, you are going to take the fall. And if you think bankers don't relish friends in high places, you have not been to any high places lately. Take a look at the following charts.

Key interest rates
December 1994 through Dec. 14, 2004

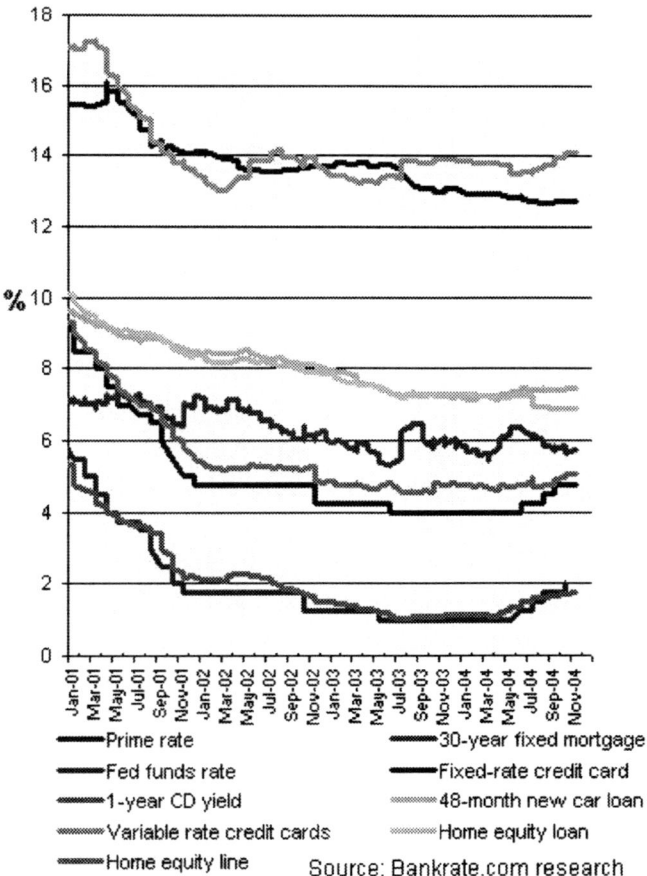

Key interest rates, 2001-2004

The Fed (red line) cut rates 13 times in response to the recession, dot-com collapses and terror attacks. With the economy strengthening, the Fed began raising rates in June.
Jan. 1, 2001 - Nov. 10, 2004

- Prime rate
- Fed funds rate
- 1-year CD yield
- Variable rate credit cards
- Home equity line
- 30-year fixed mortgage
- Fixed-rate credit card
- 48-month new car loan
- Home equity loan

Source: Bankrate.com research

Note: The Fed funds rate beginning at number 6 is the darker of the two in the legend; therefore, there is no red line.

The second chart shows how several key interest rates have moved between 2001 and 2004, a definite period of falling inflation or what many economists refer to as disinflation. The trend has certainly been downward. But notice the top two lines. The darker of the two tracks the fixed credit card rate, and the lighter 48-month new car loan rates. Like the other important rates, credit card rates have fallen over the period, but there is a huge spread between the base rates on credit cards and the others. That's called, in case you don't know, convenience. Just as things always cost more at the local convenience store, you pay up for the so-called luxury of having those cards in your pocket.

What many are also unaware of is those credit card agreements you sign when you agree to accept a credit card has in the very fine print a provision that says if you are late three times in a row with your payments, the rates will automatically jump to 21 or 22 or 24 percent. And those exorbitant rates stay in effect until you have made at least six consecutive payments on time and then you have to request that they be lowered to their original rate when you took out the card. The word request is critical and it is no exaggeration because even then the credit card company can use its own discretion about honoring your request.

Another little nasty credit card trick bankers play on the unsuspecting and the innocent is they usually incorporate their card companies in states that allow the highest interest rates. Many states have usury laws stating the maximum interest rate creditors can charge. In California, say, that rate is 19 percent. So any business within the state can't exceed those charges, so what these credit card companies do is moor their credit card home offices in, say, South Dakota that may allow a maximum rate of 24 percent. That way it can charge tardy credit card holders who live and work and play in California the higher rate without bumping up against California officials.

This brooks an interesting point. Who is most likely to fall prey to this chicanery, the wealthy or the not so wealthy, the informed or the uninformed? South Dakota may seek the jobs and economic impetus that locating the credit card company there brings. That's called politics. It's certainly one way to induce businesses to set-up shop there. So all this talk about level playing fields is just that—talk. To put it another way, one might say all is fair in love, war and banking. What you need to know is this: The Federal Reserve Bank sets what's called the federal funds rate and those changes affect what is called the short-end of the yield curve (We'll discuss more about the yield curve later.), but not all rates move lock step with the federal funds rate. Mortgage rates, for example, represent long-term debt and the long end of the yield curve. So mortgage rates are more aligned with moves in the long-term bond market. Other products, and that's exactly what they are, products, like credit cards, and you can thank the bankers for this one, have a built-in delay before reflecting federal reserve rate changes. Many would suggest, however, that the delay has a much stronger bias as it were to the downside than to the upside when rates change.

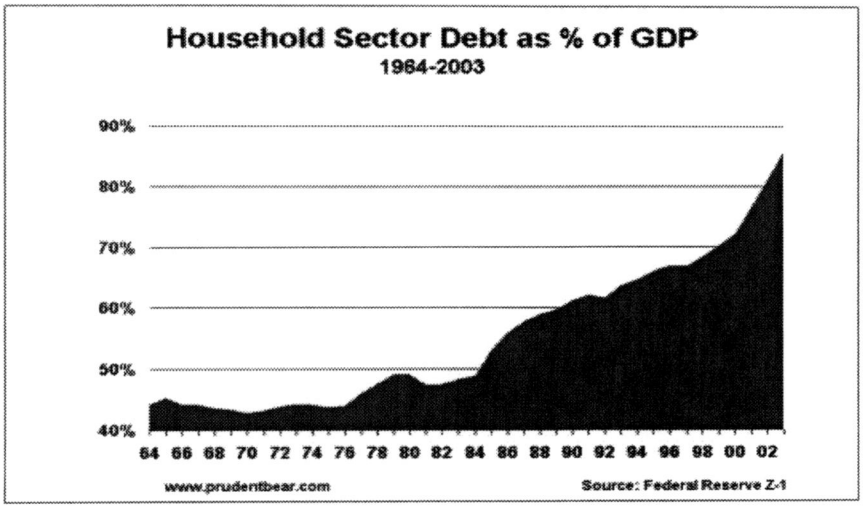

Though this chart only goes until 2003 with the borrowing and spending binge consumers have been on owing to the historically low interest rates, you get the picture.

The other side of household debt is a low savings rate. U.S. personal savings rate is at an all time low. See the chart below to determine just how low.

The point here credit represents a double-edged, sharpened blade. Properly used is can be productive; improperly used it can be destructive, a notion far too many consumers and investors fail to grasp. And that brings us full circle to creativity. Like the old bromide about being careful what you wish for, when it comes to credit you need to be mindful of what you're creating. You just may live to loathe the results. When you carry a balance on a credit card you have just forfeited control. When you pay your credit cards off every month, you're calling the shots. Which do you prefer?

We've said that bankers have friends in high places. Voltaire put it a little differently. If you spot a banker jumping out of the window, the famous French philosopher once noted, it's not a bad idea to follow because there is surely a profit in it.

CHAPTER TWO

I like men who have a future and women who have a past.

Oscar Wilde

EQUITIES

Wilde could have easily been talking about the stock market, that great discounter of the future with an illustrious, historical past. The term equities is, in case you're wondering, just another name for stocks. What was it Kris Kristofferson, in his classic song, "Bobby McGee" said: "Freedom is just another name for nothing left to lose." (Given the terrible bear market between the spring of 2000 and 2003 many people might just be thinking the same thing about equities or stocks. I hope you're not among them.)

Lots of things masquerade by other names: Superman as Clark Kent, Don Diego Vega as Zorro, Dan Rather as a journalist, Bill Clinton as President, George Dubya as a conservative. I once knew a buccaneer who masqueraded as a surgeon. So let's get that out of the way now. If I told you up front that there are all kinds of stocks (equities), common stocks, preferred stocks, convertible preferred stocks, you'd probably snap this book (sorry, manual!) shut and pickup *National Enquirer* or *People* magazine for some real serious reading. So I am not going to tell you that there are other kinds of equities besides common stocks, at least not for now.

Stocks represent ownership. And later on you'll learn if you don't already know, bonds represent debt or a loan. But that's getting ahead of our story. If you own 100 shares of ABC Corporation, you own a piece of the company, however infinitesimal. According to Finance 101, the only obligation that ABC Corporation has to you is, if they can, run the company so as it generates a profit and thereby push up the company's earnings and, if it's a publicly traded firm, stock price. In other words, in the popular vernacular of the business world, add value. Think of it as sort of a marriage; wasn't that what marriage was supposed to do for your life, add value? You were supposed to be better together than either one was apart. (OK, you can stop all that eye rolling!)

Though specific recommendations are not one of the purposes of this manual, an example of adding value might help. Johnson & Johnson, the huge pharmaceutical firm that sells everything from Band Aids to biotechnology, has enjoyed 70 consecutive years of increased sales and along the way increased its dividend 41 consecutive years to the delight of long-term shareholders. How many employees do you know who have received, however small, 41 consecutive years of pay hikes?

We may be getting a bit ahead of ourselves here, but as the saying goes: a lean dog can run a long race. As you'll find out in the next chapter on bonds, shareholders and bondholders don't always share the same interests. During the great 1990s bull market in equities that ended in 2000, companies went on a capital-spending spree, ramping up efforts to expand market share and profits. Rising profits usually translate into rising earnings and rising earnings usually equal rising share prices. Capital spending or "cap ex" as it's called on The Street, may help the economy and it may help create new jobs, but it isn't without its risks. But here is the point: When companies start tossing around their cash to expand, in general they are making a decision that favors shareholders. If you followed the stock market even vaguely during the booming 1990s you know capital gains not dividends were all the rage. You also know that many companies borrowed heavily to keep expanding. Think leverage here.

The stock market is hardly any different from anything else in life in that what goes around has a tendency to come around. Back in 2000 before the crash many companies were spending their excess capital because the belief then was corporate heads knew best. Only problem was many of those corporate chieftains mistakenly believed the Internet bubble would never burst, so they poured tons of money into fiber optics, glutting the

marketplace instead of returning much of that money to shareholders in the form of increased dividends or special payouts. And by now you know the rest of the story.

Now fast forward to the energy crunch of 2004-05 when oil companies were booking those "obscene profits." Many of the big oil firms were buying back their stocks with a fury, raising shareholders' value just as Business 101 says corporations should. Congress in its infinite wisdom called for an investigation, claiming oil companies were not reinvesting much of that money. Well, when do you want to reinvest money when prices are high and future returns of those profits will be low or when prices are low and future return on those invested funds will be high? The point here is only elected bureaucrats want to have it both ways.

On the other hand, when recoveries and expansions run short of steam, and they always do, or get overdone, companies begin to reel in their spending; preserving their cash and repairing if need be their balance sheets. Such action is a vote in favor of bondholders. According to data from the Federal Reserve, non-financial U.S. corporations nearly doubled their liquid assets in the seven years between 1997 and 2004 with most of the cash buildup coming after the stock market ran out of gas. Sitting on large chunks of cash reflects just how risk adverse companies became once the skim came off the stock market milk. Telecom and high-technology companies were some of the biggest spenders during the go-go 1990s. By mid-2004, however, many of these same companies, those lucky enough to have survived, were among the born-again thrifty. According to the credit rating agency Moody's, by mid-2004 almost one third of the 100 companies they ranked top cash holders were telecom and technology firms, the same firms we mentioned above who were spending on fiber optics during the bull market like there would be no reckoning.

Learn right here, however, that there are many wonderfully run and wonderfully profitable firms in America and elsewhere that are privately owned. Learn right here also most companies start out as private firms and many stay that way. Firms go public for various reasons, one of the main ones being increasing their exposure so they can raise capital or money. Money, capital, cash, just as in your household, is a company's lifeblood; who cares if you have a wonderful product if you can't sell it and make a profit? Yes, we know that the term profit for some is a no-no. But if you think about it, your paycheck is really an example of your profit after all those hours you put in. Anyone out there who wishes to work for free phone my agent; I have a big back yard that needs to be spruced up, not to mention dusting some shelves, hauling away some trash and mopping some floors periodically.

Another way to view stocks is they can be a way of multiplying yourself. You can only work so many jobs in one day. But it's possible by owning stocks, assuming the corporation does well, for you to participate in both growth and income, assuming that the company pays a dividend. None of this, however, comes without risk, but we'll cover risk in a separate chapter.

If you were paying attention during the big bull market of the late 1990s, you probably heard (Lord knows they repeated it enough!) that equities were the only way to ensure that you would have the kind of retirement everyone dreams of. Well, that may still turn out to be true. But during those bubbly years equities became a surrogate for savings, something they were never meant to be. Savings seldom fluctuate in value, stock values do. With savings you are usually guaranteed to get your initial investment or principle back, not so with stocks. It was all advertised as a one-way, risk free journey to everyone's own private retirement Shangri-La. But then, as usually happens when things get so one-sided and take on the patina of absolute certainty, someone tosses not one but half a dozen flies in the old investment salve. We could single several of the villains out, but suffice it to just list the initials of one, Alan Greenspan. More on Dr. Greenspan and his famous put option later.

Equities historically have returned about 11 percent per annum for the past 75 years or so. That's been the nominal return. Nominal is before you calculate in inflation. The real return has been about 8 percent for those years, and about 4.5 percent of that came from dividends. Quibblers might quibble that those numbers are a tad high or a tad low, but that's what quibblers do—quibble. You get the point. Those 35-plus percent annual returns investors were logging in the late 1990s were an historical anomaly. Yes, many stocks, usually more mature companies, pay dividends. Again, if you were around and paying attention during the bull market years of the 1990s, when stock returns were running from 25 percent to 35 percent or even higher per annum, the prospect of logging 8 or even 11 percent a year was about as attractive as a bad case of *tinea cruris* in July. Dividends at that time were the Rodney Dangerfields of investing; they didn't warrant any respect so the perceived wisdom went.

Corporations are in business to make money or create earnings. What do corporations do with those earnings? Usually, one of two or three things: reinvest them back into the company to gain more market share or maintain the business. Or they can buy back their own shares possibly rewarding stockholders by pushing up the stock's price. During the bull market of the 1990s many companies took another tack, reinvesting their earnings back into the stock market (Why not, it was only going to go higher?) to goose up revenues. And like any self-fulfilling deal it worked for a while. Still another option is the corporation can distribute cash to their shareholders in the form of dividends. And like most things in life, giving some of their earnings back to shareholders in the form of cash dividends waxes and wanes in popularity. During the 1990s it waxed pretty badly as capital gains became the rage.

In the parlance of the Street whenever you buy something and hope that it will go up in value or appreciate, we say you are long. To put it in other terms, when you got married, if you ever did, you were initially long that relationship; you wanted it to get better or appreciate. Whether it did is another question. In short, anything you want to appreciate or go up in value you're long. So if you purchase 100 shares of a stock at $10, hoping it will double or triple before next Friday, dreams do sometimes come true, you are long that stock or position. It's just a little nomenclature.

Now buying individual stocks is not that difficult. You just open a brokerage account, sign an agreement to respect arbitration should you have a dispute and you're off to the Wall Street parade. There are basically two types of accounts, cash and margin. With the first it's pretty self-explanatory; you purchase some stock and you have three business days to pay for the purchase in cash. With margin accounts, you can borrow at least one half of the amount of your purchase. Here is an example. You buy 200 shares of XCA for $20 a share. In a cash account you have to pay $4,000, not including commissions, to settle up within three business days. Saturdays, Sundays and holidays don't count as business days. With a margin account you could borrow from the broker up to $2,000 of the purchase price, paying what's called in the industry broker call rate interest on the two grand you borrowed. So you'd only have to come out of pocket with two grand and you'd pay monthly interest on the other two grand you borrowed until you closed out the trade. Or, and pay attention here, it was closed out for you.

Now margin, like credit, can be a double-edged blade. It allows you to use leverage. You are essentially controlling in the above example with a margin account $4,000 worth of stock with only $2,000 out of pocket, not including the charges for interest on your loan. Say the stock soars in six weeks to $30 a share and you sell. You get $6,000 minus the $2,000 you borrowed plus whatever carrying costs you had to pay in interest charges, and the rest is yours. Say in your initial cash account $2,000 was your entire grubstake; you would have been able to buy only 100 shares that later rallied from $20 to $30 a share and you sold, pocketing a $10 gain times the 100 shares you bought for a profit, again minus commissions, no free lunches allowed, $1,000. That's' roughly a 50 percent return on your money. With margin, however, your return even after commissions and interest expenses would be close to $2,000. Say it was $1,800. Since you initially put up only $2,000 out of pocket and you made $1,800 that's close to a 90 percent return.

Now if the stock you bought in your cash account at $20 immediately tanks and goes down to $10, you got a problem. But in your margin account you got a nightmare. Loans have covenants. That means the borrower agrees to keep the loan in good standing by not allowing it to fall in value below a certain level. Who sets the level, the broker? Yes, it's in that margin agreement you so blithely signed. You originally had 200 shares worth $4,000, but you borrowed $2,000 of those 4,000 dollars. Now you have 200 shares worth only $2,000 and you still owe the broker the $2,000 you borrowed to make the transaction in the first place. The broker sees your collateral sinking in value and knows that his loan is at greater risk. What happens if the stock goes down further, possibly even to zero? So the broker is going to ask you to put up more collateral and he's going to ask you to put it up immediately. It is what's known in the business as a margin call. You either have to come up with more cash or more acceptable collateral such as other stocks or securities or the broker will liquidate your position and take the money you have in the account to protect his loan. You agree to give the broker the legal power to do just that when you sign a margin agreement.

Now just for the drill, imagine a daisy chain. The broker usually borrows the money he lends to you from a bank, tacking on a pittance to cover his own borrowing costs to ensure a profit, and then lends the money to you. The broker is usually what is known as a bank's best customer, so the broker can borrow money from the bank at lower rates than you and I can. (Forget all that equality stuff they toss around in civics classes; this is the real world!) The bank can raise the rate it lends to the broker just as the broker can raise the rate he lends to you and me. And if things get dicey enough, the bank can call the loan from the broker, or ask for more collateral, just as the broker can call the loan from you and me or ask for more collateral, setting off a chain reaction.

Now for a moment stick on your history caps and think back to the 1920s when you could purchase stocks using 90 percent margin, something most people who buy homes can do today. When the crash came, the banks started calling in their broker loans and the brokers started liquidating their customers' accounts to meet the call because who in their right mind is going to keep putting up more capital, assuming they even have it to put up, if prices keep falling? And that's just what stock prices did, kept falling. Between September 1929 when the DJIA topped out at 381 and July of 1932 when it bottomed at just 44, despite a few modest bear market rallies along the way, it was a complete bloodbath. And incidentally, though it happened via a somewhat different mechanism, it has occurred in real estate.

Go back and look at real estate foreclosures in Colorado and Texas in the early 1980s when oil prices tanked. So keep this in mind. Though only a brief discussion of a complex subject, owning stocks on margin may be fine during a bull market when nearly everything in site is going up. Owning stocks on margin when the big bad bear arrives, however, is altogether another thing. And mark down this point: the big bad bear always shows up; the only question is when. Only fools and new-paradigm converts believe otherwise.

At the risk (there's that word again!) of boring you here are some things you need to know. Market capitalization, what in the world is that? Simply stated, the number of shares publicly traded multiplied times the share price is the definition of market capitalization. So it stands to reason that some firms have larger allocations of shares trading and trade at a higher price than other firms. Think Proctor and Gamble or General Electric, two behemoths with international markets. Then think of some small start-up company with only one product and a narrow market and only a few million outstanding shares trading everyday. Now you have the definition of two types of publicly traded firms, one quite large (large capitalization or large-cap), the other one quite small (small capitalization or small cap). As a rule smaller companies are more risky but tend to grow faster than their big brethren counterparts. So if there are small cap and large cap companies it stands to reason there must be a mid-cap and there is. So don't let the jargon get you. And when we get to the chapter on mutual funds you will discover that there are funds that reflect this breakdown.

Now just to make things a bit more complicated than they need to be (We're just kidding!) here's a few examples. On December 27, 1999, Microsoft, the world's largest company, had a market capitalization of $615 billion dollars. Today Microsoft's market capitalization is less than half that. Back then MSFT traded right at $60 a share; today it trades at $28. So a lot of value disappeared in the intervening years. For Cisco Systems the damage is even worst. In early 2000 just before the stock market sold off with the bursting of the technology bubble Cisco enjoyed a market capitalization of $548 billion. The stock traded above $80 near its peak; today you can purchase it for less than $17. That's an 80 percent drop in market capitalization and a whole passel of shareholder value vaporized.

Imagine the same thing happening to home prices. Now you know why people fear big bear markets. And big bear markets can occur in any asset class, not just equities. If you bought Cisco or Microsoft near their tops, you're still under water five full years later assuming you hung on. So learn this and learn it now; there is no such thing as zero risk. Learn too that timing matters.

And here are a few tidbits that may help you when we get to the section on mutual funds and discuss sector funds.

■ Consumer stocks usually experience earnings explosions in lower priced-oil and lower-inflation economies.

■ Small cap stocks tend to do better when borrowing costs are low and credit is plentiful.

■ Easy credit and strong currency favor small caps.

■ Large caps usually enjoy easier access to credit markets and tend to do better when times are slow and the economy dragging.

■ In general the stock market tends to do better when the yield curve is steep (See chapter on yield curve).

CHAPTER THREE

They know enough who know how to learn.

John Adams

BONDS & CHEWING GUM

When your chewing gum loses its flavor stuck on the bedpost overnight, you might want to start looking at bonds. Even with slight exposure to air, flavor can recede, and quickly. With heavy exposure, well, you get the idea. That's the lesson equity investors learned the hard way in this last big, bad, bear market in stocks after the market bubble burst. Value can disappear faster than a lot of college freshmen can organize their time or correctly pronounce rovalf; that's flavor spelled backwards.

With bonds, however, like most things in life, timing can be everything. But first a little background. Bonds represent debt, in other words a loan. Bonds are usually issued (sold) by corporations and governments, federal, state or local. State and local governments masquerade by another name, municipalities. The city of Chicago is a municipality. Orange County, California is a municipality. (Remember them, in the mid-1990s the county went bankrupt, but that's for another time.).

Your local department of water and power is a municipality. Out here in the wooly and Wild West of Southern California, the Los Angeles Department of Water and Power has issued enough bonds over the years to choke several bond traders. (Yes, bonds get traded just like stocks.) All can, and most do, issue bonds to raise money for various needs, like building school cafeterias or repairing streets and water mains and sewers. Municipalities have the power to tax and spend. And you thought only the state and federal governments could do that. For the record, just about any entity that has taxing and spending power has the power to issue or sell municipal securities. A bond is a security. A stock is a security. The government has an agency called the Security and Exchange Commission or SEC that is charged with riding herd on securities and supposedly those who deal in and sell them. The SEC has many functions, but in short, one of them, like one of cable television's biggest blowhards, Bill O' Reilly on Fox News, is the SEC is suppose to be looking out for you, the little guy and gal.

So where, you may be thinking, does the loan part come in? If you've ever used a credit card (and I'm betting you have), it doesn't matter what you used it for, to buy something, pay your taxes or get cash, the company issuing the credit card just made YOU a loan. Did they make you an interest-free loan? If you answered yes, do me a favor: send me the name of the favorite stuff you like to imbibe. It must be potent. That's right; they charged you a fee, interest, for the privilege. And sometimes they charge you both. Well, it's the same thing in the bond world, only this time you and I, if we decide to purchase a corporation's or a government's bonds, are making the loan and charging the interest. Call it a little game of table reversing. Sounds good doesn't it. And it can be.

But there are more than a few caveats here, and the one I keep repeating throughout this book (sorry, manual!) is: whenever you see yin trucking down the pike, remember yang can't be far behind. If you haven't figured it out by now, this is another way of saying, despite the myriad do-gooders and the social dreamers, there's no such thing as a free lunch. There never was and never will be. Just remember, if it walks like a duck, quacks like a duck, poops like a duck, it's probably not a duck. It's probably an investment banker trying to figure out some way he can cut another deal. And should one ever turn up, you'll be paying for it. Free lunches are like the advice noted investment guru Warren Buffett dished out many years ago: If you're playing poker for money and after an hour or so, you haven't figured out who the patsy is, you're it.

But let's get back to bonds. So now just suck it up and prepare to learn a little nomenclature. You had to do it in nursing and it wasn't that painful. Or was it? When bonds get issued, they are almost always issued at par. No, we haven't switched to golf. Par in bond parlance equals $1,000. I'm going to say that again: PAR IN BOND PARLANCE EQUALS $1,000. So ABC Corporation issues $10 million worth of bonds with a coupon rate of six percent and the bonds will mature in six years, not such a bad deal, all things being equal, in today's upside-down financial world. You and I open our pocketbooks to give the moths some air and decide to purchase just one bond. Leaving out brokerage fees, (I warned you about free lunches), it would cost us $1,000. Now since the coupon rate is six percent we would receive, usually on a semi-annual basis, say January and June, a big fat $60 in interest payments each year for six years. That is, we would get $30 in January and $30 in June. (And you thought this nomenclature stuff was tough.)

Remember, I told you this time we're making the loan and getting paid the interest for taking the risk. What risk? Well, you could've decided not to pay back that money you borrowed from your credit card company. You could just keep whatever junk you used the card to purchase and once the stuff loses its appeal toss it in the trash and keep on walking. Every year lots of folks do. So the risk here is the corporation that issued the bond we bought could, for any number of reasons, the most likely being cash flow problems as in too much debt, stop paying us our interest.

The unkind term for it is default, just as every year some people default on their home mortgages and their credit cards. How do we know they're not going to do that? How does your credit card company know you're not going to default on your credit card obligations? The short answer is they don't. The longer answer is they presumably did a credit rating on you before they issued the card. So does anyone do a credit check on corporations? You bet. Firms like Standard and Poor and Moody's and Fitch's, to name three. How reliable are their ratings, you want to know? Well, let's be kind and say they are better at it than, for the most part, the credit card firms.

Now let's wander a wee bit, for the sake of muddying up the bond waters even more, not to mention your brains. Who, you ask, is going to buy all of ABC Corporation's $10 million bonds? The answer is lots of folks. Anyone who wants to receive a definite amount of income for a definite period of time could find the deal attractive. Pension funds, retirees, insurance companies should come to mind and anyone who may have fixed costs. Retirees may eat bread, but they really live on income, most of it usually fixed. And that can present major difficulties, particularly in today's low interest rate environment. (More nomenclature, the Federal Funds Rate in November 2000 got lowered to 1.25 percent, the lowest it's been in 40- years. And in June 2003, it got lowered again to just 1.00 percent, a phenomenon not seen since Ike occupied the Oval Office. That means folks depending on income from Certificates of Deposit or Money Market Funds, we'll get to them a little later, start to ache when interest rates get too low.)

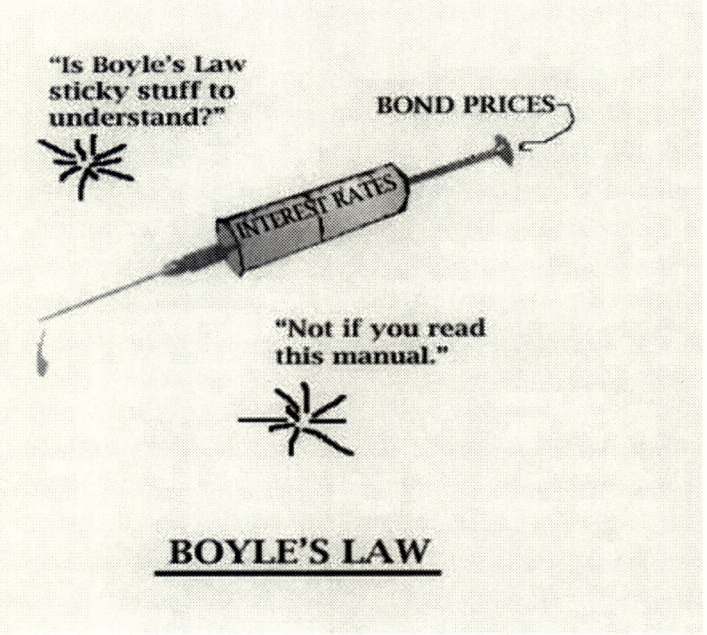

BOYLE'S LAW

Wait a minute, how did Boyle get in here? Boyle's law, if you recall your chemistry classes, (I realize a lot of you just don't want to be reminded!) deals with gases. What do gases have to do with bonds? Just this: In the 1700s Robert Boyle set out to investigate the relationship between the dry volume of an ideal gas and its pressure. (If you haven't guessed it yet, gases display certain characteristics and so do, like people, bonds.

After all, bonds have relationships, too.) Since there are four variables, temperature, volume, pressure, and quantity, that can be altered in a gas sample, whenever you want to know how one variable will affect another, the other variables must be held constant or fixed. So Boyle fixed the amount of gas and temperature to study the affect of pressure on volume. That's right: he wanted to know, simply stated, what effect pressure had on volume.

What Boyle discovered, as you all surely remember from your chemistry classes, is that increasing the pressure decreased the volume. Now let's say that again, only this time backwards: Increasing the volume decreases the pressure. So, in brief, what we have here, thanks to Sir Robert Boyle, is an inverse relationship between pressure and volume; increase one and you decrease the other. Perhaps the easiest and most familiar example for nurses is the syringe. When you stick a needle on a syringe and stick the needle into a bottle of normal saline or medicine, and pull back on the plunger, there is initially lots of pressure to overcome. As the pressure decreases inside the syringe, however, volume increases. Reverse the situation by increasing pressure and volume decreases. That's what happens when you give an injection, you increase the pressure to decrease the volume. Get it? So now you understand one of the most important characteristics about bonds. Bond prices and interest rates are inversely related; everything else being constant, any increase in interest rates will cause bonds prices to fall. So what happens if you lower interest rates? Bond prices will rally or go up.

Now here is the tough part for many would-be investors to grasp when it comes to the relationship between interest rates and bonds. Let's take that ABC bond that we bought at par or $1,000 with a six percent coupon, meaning we'd get $60 of income annually. What would happen to the price or value of our bond if interest rates dropped, say, one percent a few months after we bought it? Think pressure and volume here. If one decreases, the other increases. So here pressure equals interest rates and volume equals the price or value of our bond. So interest rates (pressure) declined and the price of the bond (volume) went up. Just like in the syringe.

Why is this important? Well, let me give you a direct answer in a round about way: If you knew or thought something was going to increase in value, exactly what many investors believe about stocks when they purchase them, would you buy it before or after it went up? So now we have at least two reasons you may want to buy bonds at sometime: One, to get the income from the interest payments and, two, the possibility that the bonds could appreciate or go up. What can make bonds go up in value or price, among other things, is falling interest rates. And just for the record, another thing that can cause bonds to go up in value or price is an improved credit rating. Whether you are talking people or governments or corporations, credit ratings get changed all the time. Some get raised, others get lowered. Who changes them? Those credit rating agencies we mentioned earlier. An improved credit rating implies less credit risk. Less credit risk implies more safety and investors will pay up for safety, especially in nettlesome times.

Just take a brief journey back through the pages of history to the Great Depression and see what deflation did to the demand for government bonds. Or why do you think they have all those automobile safety reports about how this new car or that one fares in staged auto accidents? Certain new cars are noted to be safer than others. We'll say it again: people pay up for safety. That's a basic market principle. Think 9/11 here. If the airline industry announced tomorrow that it could 100 percent guarantee safe domestic flights, but rates were going to jump 40 percent, do you think the public would balk? Probably not much.

Bonds have other characteristics: supply, coupon rate, yield and, like equities, risks. One of the biggest risks in investing in bonds you now, thanks to Boyle's law, understand: It is interest rate risk. Suppose you purchase a bond at par (remember par equals $1,000) with a six percent coupon, meaning you'll collect $60 in interest until the bond reaches maturity, say, in 10 years. This is a non-callable bond. What does that mean, just this: the corporation who issued the bond can't call or retire it before the bond's maturity date in 10 years. Is that important? It certainly could be, especially if interest rates are declining the way they have been throughout the 1990s and early in this new millennium.

Wouldn't you like to be collecting six percent when nearly everyone else is scrambling to get four percent? But back to this $1,000 bond with the six percent coupon you just bought. What happens to the price of that bond if a few months after you buy it, interest rates go up? Again, think of interest rates here as pressure in Boyle's Law and the price of your bond as volume inside that syringe. Interest rates just went up, meaning you have increased the pressure on borrowers. The price of the bond must go down, just as the volume in that syringe must decrease. That's what giving an injection is about.

Another big risk associated with buying bonds is called credit risk. (See and you thought we were finished with credit.) Remember those credit rating agencies mentioned earlier? Well, they are supposed to lessen the credit risk associated with bonds. They do this by rating the credit worthiness of the company or corporation that issued the bonds. Though ratings vary somewhat from one rating agency to another, it's really simple and straightforward. Standard and Poor uses AAA for the most creditworthy; AA for the next and so on until they get to D or bankrupt companies. (Don't laugh; some folks have made a wheel barrel of money snooping around the graveyard of defaulted bonds.) Some rating agencies will toss in a plus (+) or a minus (-) sign to further refine their ratings, the way some of your nursing professors probably did in school. Sally Smith didn't get an A and she didn't get a B on her term paper about "Neonatal Resuscitation Techniques." She received a B+, a decent grade but still far from the best. So, as Marilyn Cohen writes in her book, *The Bond Bible* (New York Institute of Finance, 2000), it's important to know your ABCs.

So what criteria do ratings agencies use to rate bonds? Well, it's a little bit like evaluating a sick patient. You look at some basics, like temperature, heart rate, blood pressure and appearance. In the bond world, it's what Ms Cohen labels as the four Cs—capacity, character, collateral and covenants. Wipe that disturbed look off your puss; you know terms are always followed by definitions or explanations. What's the bond issuer's capacity to repay the debt? Isn't that what the credit agencies or lenders want to know when they extend credit to you? What's the character of the borrower, or, in this case, the bond issuer? Character matters. Just ask all those people who wanted to impeach Bill Clinton. If you think not, imagine a patient who has a good underlying physical condition that survives an illness. How many times have you heard it said that the patient's recovery owed much to the physical condition he was in before he became ill. Or to put it another way, think about immune suppressed patients. You could easily say that the character of their credit report, to begin with, was not very good. In medicine we call it a history. Yes, history still matters; that's why we take one.

So what's the history of the corporation and how reliably have they repaid debt in the past? Collateral simply refers to what assets the corporation or company is putting up to back the debt. Does the collateral include plant and equipment or something of value that could be sold should financial difficulties arise to help recapture some of the investors' money? Covenant simply means terms. What are the terms of the deal, like who gets paid first if any difficulties pop up and can the bond be retired early. Is the bond callable? If so, when? Think terms and conditions of the contract when you think covenant. In some respects, a covenant is like a will, a setting of the terms. See there: You already know a lot about bonds. Most likely much more than when you picked up this book (or, excuse me! manual). And there's a list of websites in the index to help you find out even more.

How many different kinds of bonds are there? We just knew that question was chewing away at your investment innards. Well, at last count about 28. But we won't bore you with all the different types like those convertible into common stock or those with put options (a kind of insurance policy) attached. In the 1980s during the junk bond heydays of Michael Milkan, PIK, payment in kind, bonds were all the rage. That's a nifty deal for the bond issuer not too dissimilar from the U.S. Treasury Department since both own the printing presses. As Will Rogers years ago noted there is a difference between the return of and the return on your cash. If you think about it that is what bond and credit rating agencies are all about. How easily can you or the corporations, the borrower, repay the debt? Most retail investors put too much emphasis on the latter rather than the former.

A new (new at least to Americans; it's been around in the UK and Europe for some time) type of bond that deserves a brief mention is TIPS, Treasury Inflation Protection Securities. Issued by the U.S. Treasury for the first time in 1997, these bonds are known as index-linked paper because they afford one some protection against inflation. Here's a point you need to understand if you're going to understand the basics of bonds. Normally, bond yields contain two elements: the real rate and an inflation premium. The inflation premium calculates in what the expected rate of inflation over the life of the bond is. Because they are linked to changes in the Consumer Price Index, sometimes they are referred to, particularly overseas, as linkers. One point you need to be aware of is the adjustment for inflation is tacked on to the bonds, but it isn't payable until maturity, so you don't see any interest payments until then yet you are taxed annually on the interest. For this reason TIPS are best suited for retirement or, what financial planners call, qualified money accounts. And should you be interested, there are also municipal variants of TIPS called CPIS's.

Here are a few bullet points about TIPS:

- While buyers of TIPS don't receive interest payments until the bonds mature, the IRS computes the interest as if they do. So TIPS are best bought inside a qualified or retirement account to avoid paying taxes on them every year.

- TIPS usually trade at a premium to ordinary Treasury bonds.

- The spread (Remember that term 'cause you'll see it again!) between TIPS and regular Treasury bonds is used by bond traders to get a fix on future inflation. For example, recently 10-year TIPS were yielding 1.82 percent while 10-year Treasury bonds were yielding 4.03 percent, a spread of 2.29 percent. Traders use that spread of 2.29 percent as a proxy for where they think inflation as represented by the CPI will be over the next 10 years.

- TIPS represent a different asset class. What does that mean? Just this: TIPS are negatively correlated (Here's another term you'll be running into later.) to stocks and bonds.

- As a result TIPS help to diversify a portfolio.

- TIPS provide one form of protection against inflation. Like everything else, sometimes that insurance can be cheap and sometimes it can be expensive.

Now one another thing you know a little something about when it comes to bonds is passive and aggressive investing. Many of you, to be sure, have met passive-aggressive patients; maybe you even have passive-aggressive relatives or spouses. Now we don't want to make this any more complicated than it has to be, so pay attention. Aggressive investing in bonds usually has to do with adding value. Adding value means aggressive versus just investing in an index, the passive route. Supposedly one buys mutual funds to get professional management because professional money managers supposedly can add value. Some studies say they do, others claim the opposite. You'll have to decide for yourself.

This brings up two techniques frequently used when investing in bonds, laddering and the old barbell. The barbell is a more aggressive way to go. You simple divided your bond portfolio into two segments, one short-term and one long-term, putting half your funds in, say, bonds with maturities of 2-5 years and the other half in bonds that will mature in 20-30 years. Not a bad strategy if you believe that interest rates will decline as they did on a secular basis between 1982 and 2000. But not a good strategy if interest rates suddenly spike up as they did in 1994. (Incidentally, interest rates have gone up 15 times since 2004.) So in short, a barbell approach is a total return strategy.

With laddering you're talking about spreading your funds equally over several years. You could construct a ladder where your bonds will mature in, say, one, two, three, four and five years. Or you could ladder your funds out even further, depending on your needs and your outlook. And there is no written law that says you can't use a little of your imagination here and spread the funds out differently. Laddering is almost an automatic pilot approach, similar to indexing but not without its risks. If you ladder out too far on the yield curve and interest rates spike, your short-term bonds may not mature quick enough to make up for the lost value in your long-term bonds if inflation spikes up.

But any discussion of bonds (And remember this is just a manual; we're not trying to turn anyone here into Bill Gross!) would be faint-hearted without at least some mention of the yield curve, the subject of our next chapter. The yield curve is to bonds what sleep is to rest: it would be fairly difficult to fully enjoy one without the other.

CHAPTER FOUR

An economist is an expert who will know tomorrow why the things he predicted yesterday didn't happen today.

Laurence J. Peter

THE YIELD CURVE & SHAPE

Unfortunately time can alter one's shape. (If you haven't discovered that yet, you're probably not over 30 and I think I feel a huge dislike bubbling to the surface!) Admittedly, other factors can come into play, like laziness or inactivity or over indulgence. Folks are not the only ones who become indolent or over-indulge. Try governments and corporations. To begin to understand the yield curve, you'll need to develop an appreciation for time, shape and, yes, indulgence, including over and under.

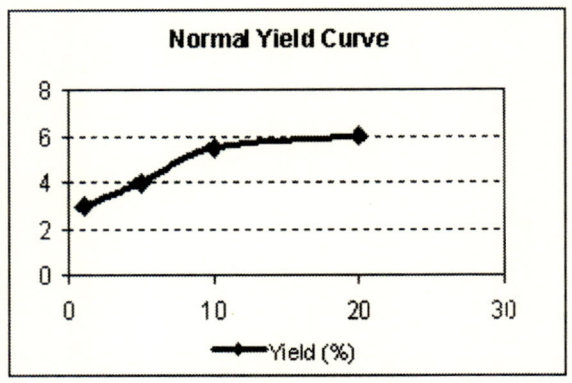

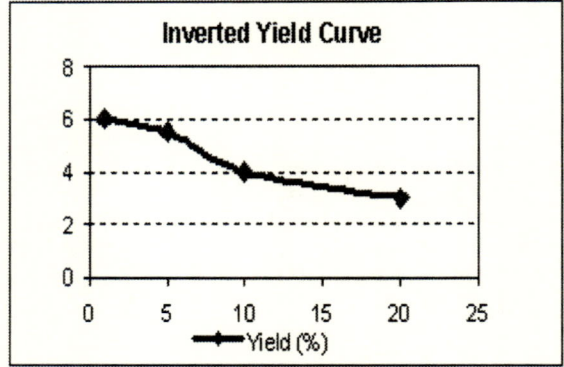

The Treasury yield curve is often used as a benchmark for other fixed income securities. The Treasury yield curve is an effective benchmark for pricing bonds and determining yields of bonds in other sectors since it is not impacted by credit risk or liquidity risk. (That should be taken with a grain of sodium chloride given the nation's current twin deficits!) On the other hand, Treasuries are backed by the full faith and credit of the U.S. government and are therefore not subject to credit risk. The Treasury market is extremely liquid, since it is the largest and most actively traded bond market.

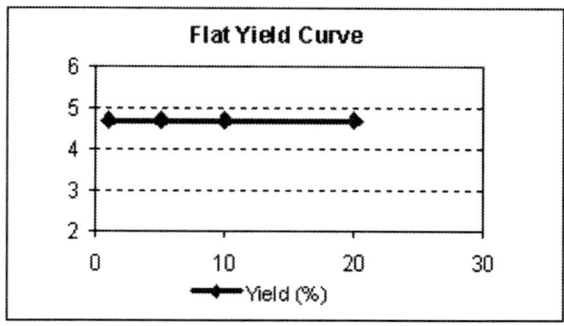

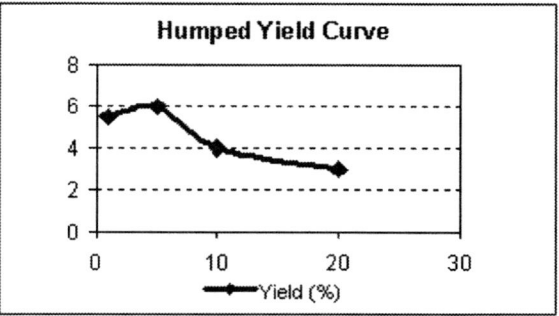

Source: Blasingham and Ellison Financial Group

Take a look at the shape of these graphs. In the world of interest rates and bonds, they truly do equal a thousand words. The horizontal axis represents time, in this case from three months to 30 years. The vertical axis represents yield. From essentially zero to eight percent. Roughly speaking from three months to about two years is known as the short end of the yield curve. And it's the short end that, incidentally, the Federal Reserve Bank can affect with its policy whenever it decides to either lower or raise interest rates.

Don't be lulled asleep here. Leaving rates unchanged can also affect the short end of the curve. Leaving rates unchanged is a decision, a statement. Remember, doing nothing is actually a decision to do something. Someone sends you an RSVP to attend a garden party. You let the date come and pass without returning your RSVP and you don't go. You've made a decision and that decision doesn't exist in a vacuum. It turns out that the cute guy with the aquamarine eyes and the stringy straw-colored hair from Central Supply, the one who keeps making eye contact at the canteen during lunch, was at the gathering asking about you.

The long end of the curve is between 20 and 30 years. So that leaves the intermediate part of the curve, the part roughly between five and 20 years, though some will dispute this. What's important for you to realize is that these three parts of the yield curve exist and the bond boys and girls, meaning the bond traders, play their game accordingly, moving in or out on the curve to take advantage of certain conditions that may arise when the Federal Reserve is anticipating changing interest rates. (Ah yes, you need to know something about the Federal Reserve just like in nursing you needed to learn the meaning of prn or bid.) As boring as this may sound, like the disco song a few years back, this can be some hot stuff. And it can be really hot stuff if you get the upcoming changes right before most investors.

The whole key to investing is what we call the Wayne Gretsky affect: skate not to where the puck is but to where you think it's going to be. In the bond world this is called the expectation theory. (We just knew you wanted to know about the expectation theory.) That takes nerve, because you're going to be pretty lonely (not to mention occasionally wrong!). And it takes some study and anticipation. If you're afraid of making a mistake or being lonely, join an online dating service or don't leave your abode everyday. Investing is not about not making mistakes; it's about making as few as possible and cutting the ones you do make early so they don't turn into your worst nightmare. The Gretsky affect is exactly what markets do; they anticipate where rates or stock prices or the economy is going to be not where either one may be at the moment. For obvious reasons this is a difficult concept for beginning investors to grasp. How many of us run around thinking much about where we're going to be in six months let alone in 10 or 20 or 30 years? Yet it is something you need to consider if you're ever going to get a decent handle on the whole investing game.

The short end of the yield curve has to do with very short term, usually up to two years, debt or interest rate obligations such as Treasury bills and Treasury notes. Treasury Notes usually run from 2 to 5 years. Remember, we mentioned the Federal Reserve a while back, well, the Federal Reserve whenever it changes interest rates, moving them up or down, it affects the short end of the curve but not the long end of the curve. The long end is most influenced by the market and the market is mostly influenced by, though some will deny this, investor psychology. The rate that the Federal Reserve in Washington usually changes is what's called the federal funds rate; that is the rate of interest that the Federal Reserve charges member banks on overnight loans. Now before you slam this manual shut in disgust, just listen up. The United States has a Federal Reserve System with an independent central bank, the one Mr. Greenspan (and now Ben Bernake, Sir G's successor**) heads up in Washington, which influences the supply of money and credit in our society through its control of bank reserves. In plain jargon, they own the printing press. Most big banks are members of the Federal Reserve System and, as such, are subject to the rules of the FOMC, the Federal Open Market Committee, the group of policy makers within the Federal Reserve.

This committee essentially controls interest rates by stipulating how much money or reserves commercial member banks have to keep on deposit. Look at it this way. Suppose you make $100 a week but only take home $80? Does that limit your spending or purchasing ability? Suppose next week you still take home $80, but the government said you have to keep $5 of that in savings or reserve? Would that affect your spending power? Of course it would. You say the government would never do that. Well, maybe they would and maybe they wouldn't; the government has rationed many things in the past, one of which is how much money or credit is available. You are not formally a member of the Federal Reserve System, so the government doesn't regulate how much money you have to save or keep in reserve. But the government does regulate via the Federal Reserve System how much money or reserves member banks have to hold. Think of it as the supply of money. Some months we all have more of it than other months, and how much we have can affect our spending or purchasing habits. So here is the important point. The United States in broken up into banking districts, 12 to be exact, and each district has a Federal Reserve Bank. There is one in San Francisco, one in Atlanta, one in Dallas, one in Boston, one in New York and so forth. And Mr. Greenspan and his committee can actually dictate policy to these member banks.

** *In January 2006 economist Ben Bernanke, a former member of the FOMC, was appointed by President Bush to replace the retiring Alan Greenspan as Fed chairman. Greenspan was appointed in 1987 by President Reagan. Bernanke chaired his first official meeting in March 2006.*

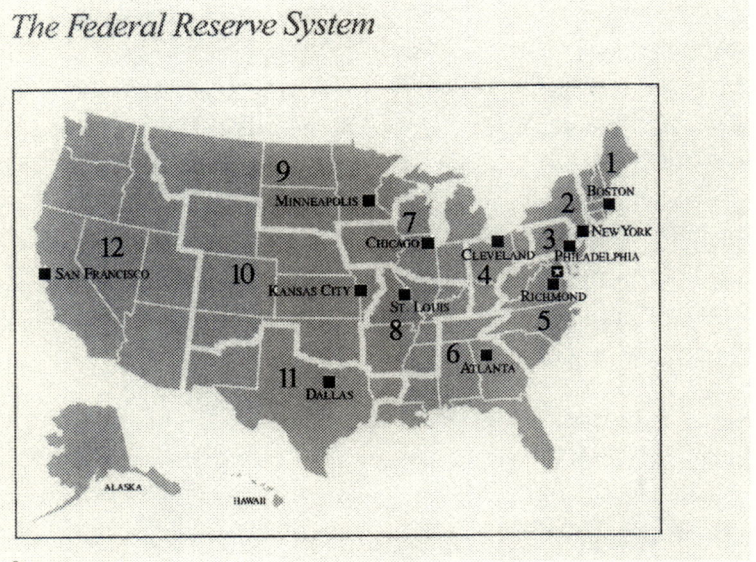

The Federal Reserve System

You didn't learn nursing in a day and you won't learn all about investing and the yield curve with one reading. But you will understand the basics. Since the short-end of the curve doesn't go out more than two years, it is considered more predictable than, say, the intermediate or long end of the curve. Think about it this way: Why do most home buyers choose a 30-year fixed mortgage rate when the average turnover rate for homes, at least in California, is about seven years? Most homebuyers could get much lower payments with a variable rate mortgage. Variable rates are tied to the short end of the yield curve and these rates go up and down fairly frequently. So there is volatility here and risk.

When a homebuyer chooses a 30-year fixed mortgage, he locks in the rate for a longer time period. Fine and good, you say. But the mortgage company charges a higher interest rate. Why? Because the mortgage company doesn't know where interest rates (and neither do you nor we) are going to be in 30 years. So the mortgage company has to be compensated for the risk or uncertainty. Get a handle on it right now that uncertainty and risk are fungible in the eyes of most investors. Interchangeable is what we mean. Who likes uncertainty? The homebuyer chose the 30-year fixed rate to avoid it. Why should the mortgage lender find uncertainty any more appetizing?

So the long end of the yield curve carries with it more risk in almost every case. Notice we didn't say volatility. Yet prices of bonds on the long end of the curve will go up or down more dramatically with changes in interest rates. Whenever inflation rears its not-so-beautiful head, (That is, unless you've been living in Japan for the decade where a little inflation is devoutly to be wished by many!) interest rates rise accordingly, creating for long-term bond owners what in most cases is their worst nightmare; the value of their bonds fall significantly. Think back to Boyle's law. Decrease the pressure, volume goes up; increase the pressure, volume goes down.

Higher interest rates equate to increased pressure on the economy. Economic output as a rule tends to decline. Some industries, financial firms, housing and construction should come readily to mind, do worse during times of higher interest rates and the long end of the bond market or the long end of the yield curve usually doesn't fare well when interest rates go up. Conventional wisdom holds that you don't get paid for the interest rate risk (Note that word risk; it's something we will cover later!) on long bonds. And for years, roughly from 1980 through 2003, you would have been paid handsomely for ignoring that piece of advice. Why? Because interest rates, not that anyone knew it for sure, in 1980 were about to enter into a long-term down trend that would take rates from the mid-teens to levels in some cases not seen in forty-plus years. Sure there were some jolts and jerks along the route; interest rates never go straight one way whether it's up or down for too long, but this was one example where the trend, as the popular saying goes, did turn out to be your friend if you were in long term bonds.

We hate to do this to you, but it's important to pick up some more vocabulary. When you purchase bonds you should have some idea about duration. In some ways duration for bond professionals is equal to beta for stock buyers. Here's the formal definition:

Duration relates to the sensitivity of a bond's price to changes in interest rates. To put it differently duration is a gauge you can use to measure how volatile your bond or bonds are to any changes in interest rates.

Let's take a 20-year bond with a coupon and duration of 15 years and interest rates decline by 100 basis points or one percent, the price of the bond will appreciate by 15 percent. And just the reverse is also true. An increase in interest rates of 100 basis points would cause the bond's price to decline by 15 percent. Now, suppose you had a whole portfolio of bonds with an average duration of 10 years. An increase or decrease of interest rates will cause the value of your bonds to go either up or down. If rates go down, your bonds increase in price and you're happy; if rates increase, your bonds decline in value and you're unhappy—that is, unless you have shorted the bonds, but that's for another time.

So this engenders a trend question of sorts. If you think the trend for interest rates is higher do you want to own bonds or a bond portfolio with a long duration? On the other hand, if you had some inkling that interest rates were headed into a long-term downward trend, you might want to lengthen the duration of your bond holdings. So professional bond managers will change the duration of their bond holdings based on what they expect interest rates to do, moving to shorter durations when they expect higher interest rates and just the opposite when they believe rates are headed down. So if you were a bond investor seeking big total returns (income plus capital gains) you might own a portfolio of long-term bonds with a longer duration to get the biggest bang for your buck. You would want the value of your portfolio to be quite sensitive to interest rate changes, but don't forget to include one of the most important parts—praying that you get the trend in interest rates right.

And speaking of trends you should note historical trends whenever possible, not that they are written in concrete. But landmarks, road signs and the like are what maps are all about. Maps and geographical borders can change. Think about all the new countries in the world that weren't there, say, 50 or 75 years ago. Recently, the European Union admitted several new countries, Slovenia and Slovakia, to name just two that didn't exist less than 25 years ago. But we still need to know something about maps and geography. So here is a historical marker for you. The Federal Funds Rate is the rate of interest on overnight loans of excess reserves among commercial banks. Since the Federal Reserve has considerable control over the availability of money, (Monopoly is the actual word that should come to mind!) or federal funds, the federal funds rate is an important indicator of monetary policy. For example, if the Federal Reserve decides to lower the fed funds rate it may be signaling an attempt to stimulate the economy by making money more freely available.

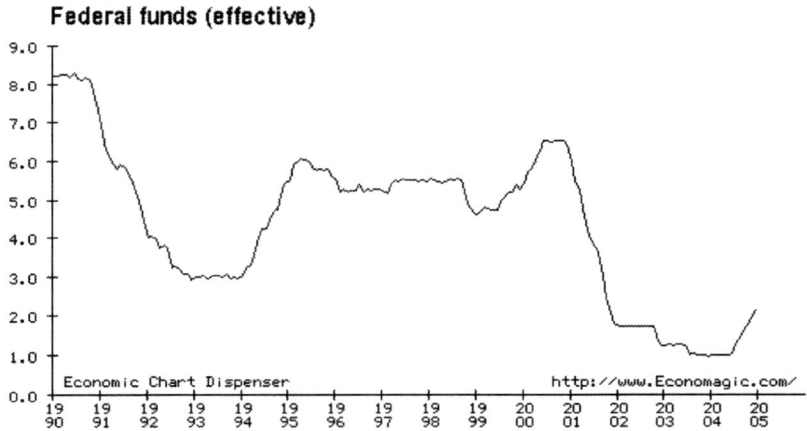

Source: Blasingham and Ellison Financial Group

In other words, it is creating credit by encouraging folks to borrow. Call it the temptation of cheap money. After all, who can resist those new cars with finance rates of one or even zero percent for five years? And just the reverse is also true. By raising the fed funds rate the Federal Reserve may be trying to slow things down a bit to prevent inflation or to keep the economy from getting too hot. (Who decides what defines too hot or too cold? They do. We'll get to who is they a bit later. But thanks for wondering.) It is really somewhat more complicated than this, but for all intents and purposes many business people and economists and even speculators follow the fed funds rate and use it as an indicator of what might happen. In short, the Fed's actions are called monetary policy. Now get this right here; there are really only two kinds of economic policies, monetary and fiscal. Monetary has to do with the creation of money and credit; the Federal Reserve controls both. Fiscal is about spending, government spending.

Raising and lowering the fed funds rate is only one ploy the Federal Reserve can use. Another method the Federal Reserve trots out from time to time is what's called open market purchases of U.S. government bonds. Simply stated, if the Federal Reserve wants to put money into the system to help stimulate the economy it goes into the market through its trading arm at the New York Federal Reserve Bank and buys bonds. Where does the Federal Reserve get the money to purchase the bonds, T&A. No, we're not talking about that kind of T&A; we're talking thin and air here; they get the money from thin air. And when the Fed wants to take money out of the system, it simply sells bonds. Either way, it's all about accounting legerdemain; no actual money changes hands. Whereas the Fed has a legal mandate to create money from thin air, if you and I try it we'd wind up in the big joint for counterfeiting. And that's exactly what it is, counterfeiting.

And now for a little history, an important subject that today has fallen into disrepute with many people who seem to care about only the here and the latest. As old Harry Truman once put it: "The only thing new today is the history you failed to learn yesterday."

The Marriner S. Eccles Federal Reserve Building that houses the Federal Reserve Bank in the nation's capitol stands imposingly along Constitution Avenue. The huge marble structure was built in the 1930s and Eccles served as Fed chairman from 1934 to 1948. Such a location for what many believe is the world's most powerful central bank in the world's most famous democracy is not without its irony. A little over 200 years old, when this nation was first born a controversy erupted about whether it should have a central bank. In 1789, just one year after the Constitution was ratified, the nation's first Secretary of the Treasury, Alexander Hamilton, the noted Federalist, urged Congress to create a national bank and Congress complied, creating in 1791 the first Bank of the United States, giving the new bank a 20-year charter and $10 million in capital, about two year's lunch money for someone like Bill Gates by today's standards. But back then it was big bucks.

Just as the old saying about true love never running smooth, this was hardly a heaven-hatched match and controversy soon erupted over what the United States would become famous for—competition. This new bank, also known as the BUS, as one chronicler has written, "served as a bank for the U.S. government, holding deposits, expanding its credit, receiving payments... and issuing notes. But it also competed with private and state-chartered banks, and acted as a restraining force on those free-wheeling rivals, which explains much of the controversy...." Not too much different from today, the first BUS pushed for a stable currency, favoring in the process lenders over borrowers (see deflation and inflation definitions), a fact that hardly sat well with farmers seeking to pay back their loans with depreciated or "cheaper" dollars.

Soon such shenanigans captured the ire of perhaps the American farmers' greatest ally, Thomas Jefferson. Jefferson was a hard currency advocate and he promptly challenged the BUS on constitutional grounds. After the War of 1812 a second central bank was established and it lasted until 1834 when hard-money advocate Andrew Jackson, a Democrat, captured the White House. For roughly the next 80 years (until 1913 when the current central bank was created) the Republic remained free from the yoke of central banking.

Some people defend central banking; others oppose it, accusing the central bank of being just another bureaucratic interloper, interfering and screwing up Americans' lives on a grand scale. Perhaps the opinion of those who most oppose a central bank is best described by economist Milton Freidman in his 1992 book, *Money Mischief Episodes in Monetary History.* Friedman laconically wrote: "Money is much too serious a matter to be left to central bankers." For some Freidman's comment is too kind, for others the terms central bankers and bureaucrats are fungible. Either way, you need to know a little bit about the Federal Reserve Bank and how it works because its actions, especially when it's controlled by Delphic-like figures such as Alan Greenspan, can have a huge impact on your life and your standard of living whether you realize it or not. So, too, do you need to get an opinion if you don't already have one; and we have ours and like the archaic, bureaucratic morass masquerading as the United Nations, we would, given our way, abolish the institution yesterday.

How would you like to be an organization or firm with no budget, hold closed meetings, subject to no audits, accountable to no one, supervised by no one, not even Congress, and literally control the entire nation's money supply in a so-called democracy where at least in part one of the basic tenets is supposed to be the peoples' right to know? No, we're not talking Mafia or drug cartel here. We're talking bank—as in central bank, the United States Federal Reserve Bank currently headed by Sir Alan Greenspan, a nearly 80-year-old former Wall Street economist and consultant whose track record there was about as mediocre as mediocre gets.

The ironies here are almost too numerous to tally. But we'll give it a try. During the 1997 Asian-crisis Greenspan grumbled about a lack of transparency among the region's banks and financial institutions. More transparency, apparently one of Greenspan's favorite terms, especially when it applies to others, judging from the number of times it crops up in his comments about solutions to economic and corporate mishaps, was needed to cleanup the mess and to prevent future troubles. Again, in 1998 when the Greenspan-led Fed rode to the rescue of Long-Term Capital Management, a hedge fund run by two Nobel-prize winning economists and some of the best so-called Wall Street brains and computer programs money could purchase, unexpectedly washed ashore on the shoals of big-time leverage.

Apparently, transparency doesn't apply when Mr. Greenspan is working behind the scenes as in his rescue of LTCM. Mindful of the Beatles' classic, "I Get a Lot of Help from My Friends," LTCM got a lot of help from their friends at the Federal Reserve. Greenspan perpetrated the hoax under the guise of a systemic financial risk. That's the inverse, in case you don't recognize it, of the too-big-to-fail argument frequently used to bail out the arrogant and the slothful. In Bob Woodruff's much acclaimed *Maestro Greenspan's Fed and the American Boom*, Woodruff recounts the story behind Fed Vice Chairman Alan Blinder's decision not to seek reappointment in 1996.

Outwardly upset at what he saw as Greenspan's iron handed control of the FOMC, Blinder felt like the odd man out, a charge, according to Woodruff, Greenspan reportedly knew was swirling about but chose to ignore. The name of Felix Rohatyn, a longtime Greenspan acquaintance and President Clinton's favorite New York investment banker, comes up as Blinder's possible replacement. Rohatyn openly coveted the position. (While Rohatyn was not appointed, he was later rewarded when Clinton named him ambassador to France, considered by many as one of the juicier Foreign Service assignments). Woodruff has Greenspan and Rohatyn renewing old friendships with Greenspan warning his old Wall Street buddy about how many evil people populate Washington D.C., normal folks who can look one straight in the eye Greenspan notes, and lie about what they have done.

Woodruff then has Greenspan proclaiming "that it is evil to lie outright." Later, however, Woodruff recalls how something President Clinton has said on the economy may be interpreted as conflicting with Greenspan's view, so Clinton has his chief economic advisor, Gene Sperling, phone Greenspan to warn him that the media might smell the makings of a story. According to Woodruff, Greenspan replies: "I'll just say a little bit this way and a little bit that, and I'll completely confuse them so there will be no story." And, as Woodruff notes, there was no story. So here apparently is a guy, Sir Alan, like his former boss, with his own definition of transparency. We cite this story not for partisan reasons, but rather to substantiate the importance of the 2Ps—politics and position. They matter and they matter mightily on your journey to investment health. But we'll get to them later.

N. B. Woodruff is the journalist nonpareil at piecing together important peoples' conversations. Woodruff has made a whole career out of it. He gets away with what even the lowest thesis students would find their theses tossed into the fire for doing, not identifying sources, just piecing together so-called conversations. This is the same Woodruff whose fiduciary responsibility as managing editor at the *Washington Post* a few years ago included directly overseeing a young female writer who turned in blatant lies and fabricated material in her stories about inner city youth and their poverty. Woodruff who likes to pen books about others shirking their responsibility was never held accountable. Unilateralism, like beauty, appears to indeed be in the gaze of the beholder.

The Greenspan-controlled Fed has been more about semantics than economics. Through his tenure investors have suffered such pathetic linguistic nonsense as "irrational exuberance," "pre-emptive strikes," "patience" "policy accommodation," and "measured pace." Baseball has its designated hitter. At the Greenspan Fed they have a designated leaker; and that role fell to Fed governor and former Princeton University economics professor Ben S. Bernanke. Like every good lackey should Bernanke spent much of 2003 zooming around the nation spewing forth deflation fears, providing Greenspan with a smoke screen to keep interest rates artificially low all the while pumping more air into the consumer debt and real estate bubbles.

It was quintessential opacity. Despite all the economic palaver about excess global capacity and a U.S. jobless recovery, the odds favoring actual deflation (the decline of all not just some prices) were about as remote as O.J. Simpson finding his estranged wife's murderer on a golf course. As his stature increased Greenspan became the Chauncey Gardner of the financial scene. Whereas Chauncey, the fictional character played superbly by Peter Sellers in the movie "Being There," said little, Greenspan mutters much. But the outcome is the same, doublespeak.

Less than one year later Bernanke was at it again, only reversing himself this time when in mid-May 2004 in Seattle he gave a speech entitled: "Gradualism. Why the Fed Tends to Move in Small Steps." Here the emphasis was on further rate hikes not cuts. So in less than one year, this astute organization headed by Father Greenspan, the keeper of all data economic, was pulling a 180-degree turn. Deflation was no longer the worry, not that it ever really was; owing to Greenspan's keeping the monetary sluice gates wide open investors were now suddenly facing rising prices on everything from energy to food to interest rates to paper products to real estate to steel.

To get a further fix on just how inaccurate Greenspan has been, the recession of the early 1990s began in July 1990 and officially ended in March 1991. Yet FOMC records from later in 1991 clearly had Greenspan muttering in August of that year about the possibility of a recession. The recession had come and gone and Sir Alan didn't get it. At $41.58 a barrel crude oil gets pretty sticky. And that's exactly what a barrel of crude was going for in early May 2004. Suddenly people found they were paying more than $2 for a gallon of gas. Now those who would tell you that on an inflation-adjusted basis that gasoline and oil was cheaper than the last time oil and gasoline prices spiked to those levels in the late 1970s and early 1980s could teach the political spin masters in Washington a trick or two. Truth is the CPI they used to calculate inflation then and the CPI they use today are about as different as popcorn and pizza.

The current CPI has been so watered down by Greenspan and others that the only people who take it seriously are agenda-flack, sycophants and the mainstream media. You could get more accurate data on inflation from an Ouija board. These people like to talk about what they call the real cost of oil, meaning you take the nominal price of a barrel of oil and subtract inflation. Nominal price minus inflation equals real price. If, however, you're using a phony gauge to gauge inflation in the first place who cares? It's one of those feel-good things people like to do to make everyone else feel less depressed as when someone dies suddenly without any warning and well-intentioned friends and relatives say: "Well, at least so-in-so didn't suffer." So what, the guy is still dead and you're still paying $2.50 a gallon at the pump with a dollar that has lost nearly half of its purchasing power in the intervening 20 or so years.

The rising cost of a barrel of crude oil doesn't happen in a vacuum. Between late September 2003 and early June 2004 crude oil prices jumped more than 50 percent. Several sectors of the economy, ones you might not readily suspect, like mining and metals, chemicals and paper start to feel the pain because fuel costs comprise a significant part of their total costs. With chemicals, for example, 60 percent of input costs are fuel related. In building materials 10 to 15 percent of costs are hitched to fuel. And here's one you probably didn't think of, cement, 25 percent of cement manufacturers' overhead is energy-related. And of course there are the obvious ones like transportation, not just yours and mine, but airlines, railway and trucking. Much of this nation's goods move overland everyday by truck and rail. So that poses a question: How do higher crude costs impact economic activity and prices? Studies have shown that every $10 increase in the oil price reduces U.S. GDP by 0.2 percent while adding 0.4 percent to inflation.

Too many investors fail to understand that moving from cash to equities or bonds or real estate or whatever is about resources. With crude oil prices at $40-plus per barrel levels and gasoline at the pump above $2 consumers are forced to move more of their resources into transportation, leaving less for other things like savings and consumption. In mid-May 2004 crude oil hit $41.85 a barrel. On June 1 the black gold hit $42.33 a barrel. An official at Wal-Mart, the eight hundred pound retail gorilla, noted that high gasoline prices were taking about $7 a week from Wal-Mart customers' pockets. That's almost $30 a month. Multiply that times Wal-Mart's huge customer base and you're easily into higher mathematics. To put it another way, economists calculate that every penny rise in gasoline prices sucks $1 billion dollars from consumers' pockets. Between January and May 2004 gasoline prices shot up 50 cents, siphoning off roughly $50 billion. And most of you know what has happened to the price of crude and gasoline during 2005.

In February 2003 Greenspan delivered a speech to the Senate Special Committee on aging proclaiming that the CPI was still overstating inflation by as much as 0.5 to 1.0 percent. During that speech Greenspan railed against the growing budget deficit and emphasized the need to cut government spending. Among the possible changes he suggested switching to a different measure of the CPI that shows lower inflation rates, claiming that the current CPI has "an upward bias that overstated inflation." The new method, he maintained, would cut the budget deficit by an estimated $40 billion. It was a clear shot across the bow of retirees and those living on a fixed income. In short, it was the Maestro Man's attempt to screw the COLA folks and help balance the budget on the backs of the elderly.

Within weeks the Fed's litany of deflation fears erupted as Bernanke took his deflation dog and pony act on the road. On June 13, 2003 bond yields hit record lows and bond prices were hovering at record highs in what would be the top of the bond market rally that actually started way back in the 1980s when government bond yields and inflation both hit 14 percent. In 1994 Greenspan again wrong-footed investors and the bond market when he unexpectedly hiked rates faster and farther than anticipated. The Maestro Man cranked up the

Fed funds rate 250 basis points in six moves over a 10 month period, catching unaware in the process Robert Citron, treasurer of Orange County, California, who had about $1.7 billion of the county's funds he'd borrowed short and invested long in the derivatives market. Long Treasury bonds dropped 25 percent of their value. When the whole thing unraveled, Orange County was bankrupt and Citron disgraced and out of a job. Unlike Long-Term Capital Management, however, Citron apparently didn't have enough friends in high enough places. And neither did Orange County and its taxpayers.

For months leading up to the stock market crash in 2000 Greenspan assured the public that the Fed stood ever ready to ease monetary policy should trouble appear on the economic horizon. All the while Mr. Greenspan was ratcheting up rates 75 basis points in 1999, tacking on another 100 basis points in 2000, to finally slow down a stock market apparently four years earlier he felt was behaving irrational. Though conceivable, a serious downturn stood little chance of happening because all the Fed had to do was tweak interest rates down a few notches and it would be Soft Landing City. (You have to understand that economists love to talk about soft and hard landings. The description alone should tell you which one they and their political brethren prefer.)

After all it had been nearly four years since he uttered his famous "irrational exuberance" tripe. The stock market barely blinked on its way to investor nirvana. The wonders of new-age productivity in all of its majestic nuances now captured the Maestro's mind. It was the economic equivalent of the trapeze performer's safety net and Greenspan, like a kid making a new discovery, took great pleasure in spreading the gospel. It was a message much of Wall Street and the retail investing public gleefully gobbled up. Who needed alchemists, the Fountain of Youth or low-carbohydrate diets? Americans had the Maestro Man and the promise of early, lavish retirements. In effect, Greenspan became Robert Young incarnate and it was abundantly clear Father Greenspan really did, his admirers believed, know best.

In January 2001 a somber Greenspan appeared before a group of bankers. His message was quickly followed by a 50 basis point drop in rates. The magnitude of the decline caught many off guard, sending the clear signal the Fed was once again behind the curve. Six weeks later the Fed decreased interest rates another 50 basis points. Those two quick consecutive rate declines turned out to be the first of 13 in all, spread over a two year period, as Greenspan and his merry band of central bankers dropped the Fed funds rate from 6.5 to a paltry 1 percent and, like a discarded lottery ticket, left it there to languish for months while the rest of the globe tried to figure out where the world's largest economy was headed next. The Big Easy might be in Louisiana, but Easy Al, briefcase in tow, was clearly ensconced in the nation's capitol.

Proponents praise Greenspan for saving the stock market after Black Monday in 1987 when the market shed 565 points in one day. Throughout 1987 interest rates and the stock market continued to rise in tandem. The up-surge in stock prices had already created an additional $1 trillion of wealth in 1986. Folks were starting to feel good again, a dangerous attribute in the eyes of many bureaucrats, while on Wall Street a takeover craze captured the Street's imagination and the nation's largest savings and loan, American Savings and Loan, was on life support pending another infusion about to expire. The whole thing smelled of money, Wall Street's sustenance and raison d'etre. So in August when Greenspan rolled in to chair his first-ever FOMC meeting, according to Woodward's account, the former clarinet player from New York expressed shock that none of the other members of the committee mentioned the stock market and the danger it posed to exciting a run-away economy.

The economy of 1987 in Greenspan's eyes was too strong, too vibrant, and, paradox of paradox, too full of itself. Though to Greenspan's mind, although no visible signs of inflation were yet on the horizon things were going too good and something had to be done. He was sure of it. On September 4, just 14 days after his first FOMC session, Greenspan convened another meeting of Fed governors, one that was a classic example of democracy inaction. Of the seven-member board two members were out of town that day and one vacancy remained yet to be filled. So with just four governors present including the Maestro Man himself, Greenspan decided to hike the discount rate 50 basis points. The stock market at first just shrugged while the DJIA continued to hover around its high slightly above 2500. Then came

Monday, October 19 and the bloodbath that obliterated $1 trillion of wealth, the same amount that it took the entire year of 1986 to build, the omniscient Father Greenspan managed to wipe out in one day.

Perhaps the most damning evidence that Father Greenspan is (and has been) running a one-man monetary show comes from former Fed governor Laurence Myers' book, *A Term at the Fed: An Insider's View*, published in July 2004. Myer served on the board from 1996 to 2002. Myer recounts after a vote by the FOMC in 1997 to hike rates, he was surprised to learn that the accompanying statements had been written before the governors met. Besides Greenspan, Myer claims, the only other input on the statements came from the director of monetary affairs. Speaking of the statements that were to be released to the press, Myer writes: "As such they did not reflect a shred of the discussions we (the committee) had just concluded." Even more telling Myer reveals: "Frankly, to this day, I do not know if I ever actually influenced a FOMC decision in my five and a half years."

So Greenspan admirers can admire away, but setting up straw men only to rescue them once they have been toppled is hardly the stuff of genius. It's the bureaucratic version of setting a fire and then helping lug in the water pails to reap the kudos. Bubble Man not Maestro is a more fitting name for a guy who has created more bubbles during his tenure than a soap factory: a stock market bubble, a real estate bubble, a Y2K bubble, a new-age bubble, a currency bubble and a bubble in consumer debt. And that brings up another point, where is that raspy-voiced Al Gore when you really need him: "Greenspan ought to resign!"

Percentage above bear market lows in each commodity

		COMMODITY	YEAR	HISTORIC LOWS BASIS NF	PRICES AT LOW	PRICE ON 1/02/04	% ABOVE LOW
1	CI	Crude Oil	1998	December 21, 1998	10.23	32.52	218%
2	PB	Pork Bellies	1999	July 12, 1999	32.1	86.9	171%
3	LH	Hogs	1998	December 14, 1998	20.7	55.42	168%
4	CT	Cotton	2001	October 26, 2001	28.2	75.07	166%
5	PL	Platinum	1998	October 30, 1998	332	811	144%
6	CC	Cocoa	2000	December 15, 2000	650	1515	133%
7	SM	Soybean Meal	1999	February 26, 1999	120	241.8	102%
8	S	Soybeans	1999	July 9, 1999	401.5	798.25	99%
9	BO	Soybean Oil	2001	February 14, 2001	14.35	28.04	95%
10	W	Wheat	1999	December 13, 1999	222.5	405.75	82%
11	LB	Lumber	2001	January 12, 2001	180.4	321	78%
12	HG	Copper	2001	November 7, 2001	60.5	104.55	73%
13	GC	Gold	1999	August 25, 1999	252.5	416.1	65%
14	KC	Coffee	2001	December 5, 2001	41.5	64.95	57%
15	O	Oats	2000	July 3, 2000	93.5	144.5	55%
16	SI	Silver	2001	November 21, 2001	401.5	597	49%
17	C	Corn	2000	August 14, 2000	174	253.25	46%
18	LC	Cattle	1996	April 26, 1996	54	73.8	37%
19	SB	Sugar	1999	May 3, 1999	4.36	5.67	30%
20	JO	Orange Juice	1997	October 10, 1997	65	60.75	-7%

Source: Past Present Futures, Santa Monica, CA. 90403

Here's a commodities chart that covers the period leading up to and after Greenspan and his crew were trying to dupe the public into buying the deflation scam. Some will no doubt argue that this was a period when the 800-pound-and-still-growing economic gorilla China was sucking up everything in site. Yes, it was and it was also a time when the U.S. dollar was tanking against many of the world's currencies.

We hate to do this to you, but it's important to your investing health and future. You have to understand that fiat money is backed only by a promise to pay as in "I promise to honor you in sickness and health… richer or poorer….until death do…" You've heard that one before. So have a lot of other folks. Money and credit creation are the hallmarks of all fiat money created booms. Credit creation, a monopoly controlled by the Federal Reserve with it garrote around the throat of money supply, is the real engine of capitalism.

Booms created by the printing of money and the extension of credit usually return to earth in one of two ways, softly or with a thud. If you seek firsthand observation just keep your gaze on what happens in China over the next few years.

Nine out of 10 soft landings occur owing to government interference, that is, they refuse to let the fever run its course. To put it another way, hard landings are the pay-me-now version and soft the pay-me-later with the hope that you'll never have to pay me at all. Which of the two do you think politicos and central bankers prefer? With soft landings come the hope that by the time the hour of reckoning does roll around these so-called public servants will have mounted their trusty steeds and ridden off into their retirement sunsets, leaving you and me, the taxpayers, conveniently behind to hold you know what.

We realize that we started this chapter talking about the yield curve and took an excursion to Federal Reserve Land, a place many see as a kind of monetary Disneyland. We didn't lose our way. To fully understand the importance of the yield curve investors need to also grasp something about the Federal Reserve, its past and how it operates. Together they can impact your financial future.

CHAPTER FIVE

Risk: simply not knowing what you're doing.

Warren Buffett

RISKS

Way back in chapter one when we quoted Will Rogers about being on the right track but not just sitting there, we were really discussing risk. The investment world, like life, is filled with risks and you need to recognize some of them. In the section on bonds we talked about interest rate risks and bonds, how rising interest rates cause bond prices to fall and vice versa. Well, here are some other risks you should at least be familiar with.

Credit, inflation, deflation, geo-political (litigation), currency, country, event, liquidity, market, sector and what we'll call the Will Rodger's risk of just sitting there, sometimes referred to as the "do-nothing" risk. Recall this is a manual not a tome. So we will discuss only a few of these risks, noting that the list is hardly exhaustive. In the high finance world of derivatives, for example, there is something called counterparty risk. But that's for another time and another manual. Let's take event risk first. What's an event? How about an earthquake or tornado or hurricane? Any of these can cause physical and personal damage. Or how about agricultural damage? Think oranges or tomatoes here. An even better example is 911. Nobody expected it. Hurricanes and tornadoes usually come with some warning, not so earthquakes.

Or take the Asian tsunami of late 2004 that killed an estimated 200,000 people. At first blush property and casualty insurance companies' stocks suffered. But because the area affected is rather isolated and has high rates of poverty many people didn't have or couldn't afford insurance. So you could say that their options were limited, in this case the option to hedge the risk.

Suppose you bought stock in a property and casualty insurer a month before 911? And suppose the company had underwritten the liability for some of the real estate that was devastated that tragic day. So would you hazard a guess that people in densely populated New York with some of the world's most expensive real estate could afford the option of buying insurance to hedge their risks. You can guess what happened to the price of that company's stock after that horrible day. And if you're even vaguely familiar with the tort system of law in America, you know about class action suits. Class actions suits often run hand in hand with events. In the case of 911 the courts ruled in late 2003 that the airline companies for the planes that the terrorists used could be held liable, opening up these firms to class action suits not only from the survivors of those who perished on the ground but also of those who were passengers that fateful morning. Still another eerie and perhaps tragic aspect of 911 exists. When those WTC towers were built back in the 1970s, some have speculated that the buildings were not as fire proof as they could have been owing to cost cutting. And when it comes to event risks, you should recall lead, paint and asbestos and oil spills and alleged defective fuel tanks on automobiles. More recently think Merck, the big pharmaceutical company, and Vioxx, the company's blockbuster drug used to treat arthritis. All of those will some day get washed out in the courts. What you as an investor need to come to grips with is this: risk is, despite the PC crowd's fantasizing to the contrary, still alive and flourishing.

Another type of risk, though it rarely occurs, is called systemic risk. In medicine we refer to it as septicemia, the infection is no longer localized but rampant throughout the entire body. Some historians would argue that the blunders of the Woodrow Wilson era, the stock market crash of 1929 and the subsequent government imposed regulations brought about a systemic risk called the Great Depression and World War II that followed. Certainly between 1918 and the 1939, much of the world fell into an economic and geo-political funk that many believe began with the collapse of Austria's largest bank.

Borrowing short and lending long, the famous carry trade technique, poses little risk and near certain profits as long as interest rates remain stable. Trouble is interest rates, like the weather, don't remain stable forever. We already alluded to the Orange County, California disaster of the early 1990s. Banks for the most part operate on just such a structure, borrowing short near the risk free rate and lending longer and riskier. As kids growing up we'd occasionally get to horsing around near bedtime and old mom would patiently warn us that if we weren't careful or, to use the legal jargon, if we didn't desist and stop, it would all end up in tears; and it occasionally did. Tears usually follow excesses and banks can and do like nearly everyone else occasionally get carried away. Recall the savings and loan crisis of the early 1990s.

When we talk about liquidity risks, we're talking about circulation. A lack of circulation in medicine causes ischemia and ischemia begets pain. If you have a stock, a house or a painting that you want to sell but nobody is buying, there is no liquidity. And if prices keep declining while you're stuck with your house or stock or painting, you can see that the end result could be quite painful. The other side of liquidity is illiquidity, and that's what falling markets do—drop prices until someone decides to step up and become a buyer. How long will that be? Well, in the 1929 stock market downturn, some equities lost 75 to 90 percent of their value before any significant buyers showed up. And in the technology bubble that ended in 2000, many of those tech stock darlings faced a similar fate. Stocks that once commanded hundreds of dollars per share now six-plus years later still trade for less than half of those prices and in some cases less than a third.

The point is, like circulation, liquidity matters. Too many investors assume that there will be buyers when they get ready to sell. And there may well be, but what price will they be willing to pay? When is the last time you either sold or bought something at fair market value in a yard sale? So systemic risks could trigger one big international yard sale, assuming anyone bothers to show up. We already mentioned Long-Term Credit Management, a hedge fund that Sir Alan Greenspan decided to bail out in the late 1990s. It was allegedly about systemic risk. More recently systemic risk concerns have cropped up surrounding two Government Sponsored Enterprises (GSE), Fannie Mae and Freddie Mac, the big government mortgage agencies. But that's a tale still in the telling.

And this brings us to something called country or emerging market risk. The United States is considered by some to be a safe haven, given this country's relative economic and social stability over its history. Yes, we have had our civil and economic disruptions, including the rather pathetic excuse for a presidential election in 2000 in Florida that gave rise to claims of ballot box stuffing. (Ballot box stuffing can take many different forms from uncounted dangling chads to poll taxes to overtly denying folks the franchise! And it's as old as elections. The rank truth is the U.S. has always experienced ballot box stuffing during its presidential elections, just less of it in less overt ways than other nations.) So the perception is that the U.S. is safer than other nations. But learn this and learn it now: all governments are corrupt; it's simply a matter of degrees. Only the dimwitted, the naïve and the politically zealous, sometimes known as statists, believe otherwise. What's important here is investors, like seamen, look for a safe port in stormy times. Much of being a safe port has to do with things like property rights and the rule of law, but that is another subject for another time, too.

Emerging markets are not considered industrialized or developed as, say, the U.S. or the UK or Germany or France or Japan. (Here the term industrialized, oddly enough, Al Gore and Ralph Nader aside, is considered a good thing!) Moreover, emerging markets have histories of political and economic turmoil, two things that make investors extremely nervous. Think stability here. Some Latin American nations during one period in the late 1990s and early 2000s changed leaders almost as often as some folks change their underwear. Governments have been known to seize the assets of foreigners as well as those of their own citizens or subjects, to use the less euphemistic term. To put a face on the risks investors can encounter in some of these emerging markets Harvard economics professor Ken Rogoff, in an article in the *Financial Times* over Memorial Day weekend 2004, noted: "We have a problem of serial default—with Brazil defaulting seven times,

Argentina five, Venezuela nine and Turkey six..." And when it comes to default these countries are not alone. In the 1990s, Mexico and Russia both defaulted on their obligations.

Crying for is much different from crying over, and in December 2001 Argentina defaulted on nearly $100 billion of its sovereign debt. As it should have, it sent ripples through the international debt markets. The possibility of loss makes investors nervous. And when investors get nervous they tend to vote with their feet. In the international world of investing this is sometimes referred to as "hot money." So be aware not all countries are the same, despite what those Brussels bureaucrats would like to have you believe. You may be able to get in, but getting out and at a decent price may prove problematic. For those of you who have been through the process, think marriage and divorce here. So ignore liquidity at your own peril.

A backdoor risk relating to emerging market debt developed after the stock market went south thanks to our illustrious central bankers at the Fed. By keeping interest rates at historically low levels, Greenspan and crew forced yield-challenged investors out farther on the limb of risk. In an attempt to cure their yield anorexia many investors flocked to emerging market debt where the spread over U.S. Treasuries offered the latest version of fool's gold. Demand pushes up prices and pushes down yields. So the spread between emerging market sovereign debt and U.S. Treasuries in January 2004 fell to seven year lows. To put this in perspective, many of these yield-starved investors were taking on greater risk and getting less return or yield for their efforts.

Another kind of risk can be called the room-full-of-measles risk or what Wall Street folks label contagion risk. You might also think of it as domino risk, one falls over and all the rest are knocked down. In other words, it's infectious. Such a stigma was associated with emerging market debt risks throughout most of the 1980s and 1990s.

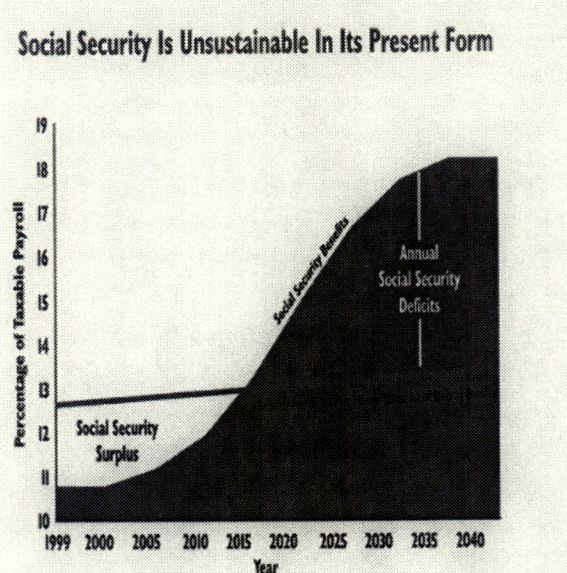

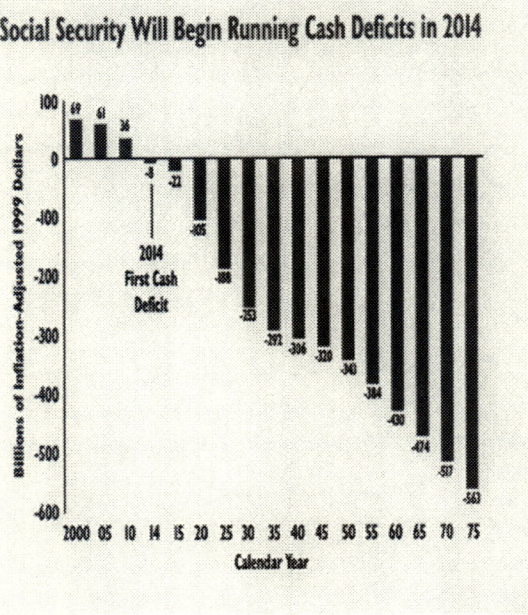

These charts are self-explanatory: Too many retirees, too few workers to support them.

With 70-plus million baby boomers in the U.S., still another risk you won't hear much about though it was indirectly referred to during the 2000 and 2004 presidential elections is longevity risk. (See above charts.) Living a long life is great for those so blessed, but for people like government officials, pension and annuity planners the distinct decline in mortality rates over the last two decades may turn out to be a monetary nightmare in waiting. Individuals worry (If they don't they should!) about running out of cash before they run out of air. Well, pension and annuity planners face a similar concern—beneficiaries living longer than expected. Perhaps you think that sounds morbid, but it's the nature of retirement planning.

Failure to plan for retirement is another risk. As more and more Americans discover that the risk of planning for their retirement is being shifted from employers and government agencies to them, it's vital to get informed. Though we hardly ever recommend anything the government does, you might want to take a gander at a new booklet offered by the Department of Labor called: *Taking the Mystery Out of Retirement Planning.* You can get a copy by calling (1 866-444-3272). It's free.

There is an old saying that is especially true when it comes to investing: "Many are called, but few chosen." Nearly everyone glibly mouths the idea that "the greater the return, the greater the risk," but few seem to really appreciate its significance. Do yourself a favor and become a member of that rather exclusive club. Much of your investment success depends on it.

CHAPTER SIX

Minor surgery is surgery someone else is having.

Joseph Cook

MUTUAL FUNDS

Mutual funds are like diseases; there are lots of them and many types. A money market fund, though its net asset value never changes, is a type of mutual fund. A bond fund, though its NAV almost never stays the same, is a mutual fund. An equity fund, though its NAV (as many 401 (k) investors discovered in the bear market that started in 2000) always changes, is a mutual fund.

A little digression may be in order. Net asset value or NAV, just what is that? Remember it's all about nomenclature. Net asset value or NAV is much like the difference between gross and net pay. Gross is what you earn, but net is, after all the deductions (And despite what the pundits would have you believe, they are ever-increasing), what you actually take home every payday. In other words, it fluctuates. Well, the NAV of mutual funds, particularly some more than others, because they are made up of a portfolio of stocks and stock prices, fluctuate daily. Bond prices change everyday, too. Bond funds have a portfolio of bonds. Bonds tend to be less volatile in their price changes than stocks depending on many factors such as interest rates, inflation, demand and the like.

It has often been asked: How much is a particular stock or mutual fund worth? Perhaps debated would be a better choice of terms here. Like most things, stocks, bonds, mutual funds are worth whatever a willing buyer is willing to pay. If you were not paying close attention when the 2000 bear market arrived, for a couple of years willing buyers were about as rare as a case of Hansen's disease. So mutual funds took a bath. Juxtapose that with the bull market during the tech mania and the number of willing buyers who readily stepped up to the buy window in great hordes. Before we go on, a little historical digression should help to elucidate the whole concept of mutual funds. So take a deep breath and plunge in. You'll find the water is just fine.

During the Great Depression people weren't willing to pay much for much of anything except the guaranteed return of their money and that usually meant U.S. Government bonds. Deflation, remember that term, has a way of driving folks to safety and conjuring worries about survival. If you were astute during the latest economic and stock market downturn, you'll have noted the run-up in prices of U.S. Treasury securities. As the prices appreciated, the yields declined. In other words, investors were shunning stocks for the most part after the stock market went south in the spring of 2000. The most basic type of mutual fund is an equity mutual fund. That means it holds mostly stocks. Call it a portfolio of stocks. Not much different from a portfolio of photographs or anything else. Both can fluctuate in value. A portfolio of stocks fluctuates in value daily whereas it might take a portfolio of photographs more time to change in value. A friend collected old photographs, much to his wife's dismay, usually storing them under the bed to collect dust. Taken by a particular nature photographer, the pictures were old black and whites. Many years later, after repeated but unsuccessful attempts by his wife to toss them out, he learned the collection was worth hundreds of thousands of dollars. That is what a lot of investors hope their mutual funds will do over time.

So how many types of funds are there? Recall the line from Elizabeth Barrett Browning's famous poem: "How Do I Love Thee?" Too many to count is the reasonable reply. But by most assessments at the top of the last great bull market the number exceeded 8,400 mutual funds. To state that number differently, those mutual funds represent a $7,000 billion industry, a number that's probably not even comprehensible to astronomers. Mutual funds first experienced the investment dawn in the 1920s. Back then they were called Investment Trusts. According to one source, at the top of the 1929 bull market there were 450 such trusts with $3 billion of the public's money and new ones were being formed at the rate of one per day. The idea back then was the same as it is today: make available a piece of the American Dream to every man. In today's PC world it would be everyman and woman. In the 1920s fund holders, like their 1990s counterparts, subscribed to the safety in numbers principal. Back then, as they would do 70 years later, shareholders believed their savvy mutual fund managers could and would protect them from any market debacle. In the investment world the idea that professional management can add value is called *alpha*. It's a concept still hotly debated.

Interest in the new funds became so strong that by 1928, the *Saturday Evening Post* observed: "It is hardly possible to find enough experienced operators," a fact that would repeat itself 70 years later when most funds were being managed by thirty year olds with still wet ink on their MBA degrees. So fast were these new investment trusts being launched, as one historian of the period noted, "promoters were having some difficulty finding distinctive names for their organizations." Seventy years later during the tech bubble anything with the word tech in it was distinctive, or so, as fate would have it, the public believed. The earmark of any mania is the belief that the public's appetite will prove insatiable. On Wall Street the axiom that best expresses that belief is: "When the ducks are quacking, feed 'em!"

After the 1929 meltdown, it would be another 40 years before the investing public witnessed that number of funds again. As one observer put it: "In 1940 only an oddball would buy a stock mutual fund and fewer than 300,000 oddballs" did. Not until the 1960s did mutual funds regain any semblance of their earlier popularity. In the late 1960s, one in four American adults owned funds. The bull market of the '60s revamped their popularity. And like their not too distant brethren, life insurance policies, mutual funds were hawked by moonlighting shoe salesmen and teachers door-to-door. Between 1965 and 1970 mutual funds more than doubled, going from 150 to 350. Hotshot money managers cropped like spring flowers. Names like Fred Mates, Gerald Tsai and William O'Neill, later the founder of *Investor's Business Daily*, all contributed mightily to what became known as the "go-go years." Proliferation may not in itself translate into overdone, but in 1977 there were only 503 no-load funds. As of March 2004 that number exceeded 2,500.

Back in the 1970s, only 5 percent of U.S. households owned mutual funds; today better than 50 percent do. Another way to look at the growth in mutual funds is in 1985 only about 40 international funds existed; by 2000 the number was close to 1,900. Take Pakistan, a country only 57 years old. Between 2000 and mid-2004 the Karachi Stock Exchange shot up nearly 180 percent, setting the stage for the launch of six new mutual funds to go with the already existing 38 closed-end funds and 10 mutual funds offering investors a way to play the equity game in that country. To put a face on it closer to home, in 2000 an estimated 83 million Americans in 48 million households owned mutual funds, representing nearly 50 percent of all U.S. households. Two things should become abundantly clear here: mutual funds have sex appeal and the mutual fund industry is big, big business.

So if 8,400 sounds like a large number, it is. It is also a confusing number that investors have to choose from. The question becomes how does the individual confront such a daunting task? And the answer for the most part is most investors don't; they just purchase the most popular or the latest high-flying fund, usually basing their decision on the latest performance figures. Or worse yet they talk to someone at the water cooler who knows a guy who had a friend whose cousin had his car repaired by a one-armed mechanic who made a bundle in the New Low Carbohydrate Maximum Protein biotech hedge fund. And the mechanic it later comes to light learned about the fund from his barber who was tipped off by his chiropodist. Now about those performance figures, they are often fed by the rating agencies such as Morningstar and Value Line and a host of financial magazines such as *Money* and *Kiplinger* that regularly cough up financial advice aimed at the proletariat.

At the beginning of this manual you were warned about terminology. To get a handle on mutual funds, you need to brush up on some terminology. We told you earlier about large capitalization and small capitalization stocks. Well, if there is large cap and small cap, there must also be mid-cap stocks. The same is true for mutual funds which, remember, purchase stocks. Then there are growth stocks, value stocks and a whole lot of terrain in between. So mutual funds get categorized and this is one way of doing it; they could be a growth mutual fund, a value mutual fund and so forth. They could claim to be a large cap, a small cap or a mid-cap mutual fund. And according to their charter, every mutual fund is required by the Securities and Exchange Commission to have a charter; they are supposed to stick to their investment knitting. We say suppose to because they don't always and some funds got into trouble during the bull market just past for what is called "style drift." Simply put, they may have declared themselves to be value funds, or growth and income funds, but were tempted by the run-up in technology stocks to invest most of their shareholders' money there, a clear violation of their charter.

So aside from performance, another important question when selecting a mutual fund is just what kind of mutual fund is it—large cap, small cap, mid-cap, growth, value or whatever? Since small companies historically grow faster than older, more established behemoths, most small cap funds are growth funds. High growth is fine, but high growth can also carry with it high risk. Think biotechnology. Biotechnology companies are usually cash-dependent, one-product small start-up firms that can hit either home runs or strike out faster than spelling bee contestants can spell onomatopoeia. Others can just sort of sop around for years, displaying no snap, crackle or pop, never quite matching their promise and yet never doing so poorly as to go under. So while a biotechnology fund would and should be considered a growth fund, it also would and should be considered a sector fun, since biotechnology is a particular sector. So now you know that a growth fund could be a sector fund and a sector fund could be a growth fund. But not all growth funds are sector funds and not all sector funds are growth funds. If it all sounds a bit confusing, stick around; it gets worse.

A lot of sectors are not necessarily high growth areas. What do we mean by high versus low or moderate growth? Well, a sector with the potential to grow at 30 or 40 percent a year is high growth versus a sector with an historical growth rate of, say, 4 or 5 percent. Think retail or energy. Both represent certain sectors of the economy. But neither sector is growing as fast as or has the potential to grow as fast as, say, technology. It is technology, after all, many argue, that allows for increased productivity and increased productivity is important because it can allow for wages to increase without causing inflation. Just ask former Federal Reserve Chairman Alan Greenspan; he'll be glad to confirm that point. Yet technology has contributed and does contribute in some ways to the growth of both retail and energy. So what are some other sectors: well, utilities, communication, capital goods, transportation, health care, housing, media, natural resources, to name a few.

So here is a question? What category would a fund fall into if it invested in all of the above-named sectors? In other words, if you bought some shares of companies in all of these sectors, what type of fund would you own? Hybrid should come to mind. But if all of the stocks or companies it purchased were large capitalization firms, it would probably be called a large cap growth fund. If all the stocks in this group paid particularly high dividends compared to the overall market, then it might be a large cap dividend or growth and income fund. Incidentally, most dividends are paid out by larger rather than smaller firms because smaller firms tend to need the capital to fuel future growth. Think retained earnings. Do you want to retain some of your earnings to buy a bigger, better house or car? That could be considered growth. And unless you're a cancer or an environmental mole, few folks really oppose growth. Think wages and purchasing power and creature comforts here. Would you like to have more of all three?

Notice that the categorizing of these funds—large cap, small cap, balance, value, growth—says nothing about risk. In other words, what you as an investor should focus on is risk versus reward versus segment or sector. By now you ought to have figured out that some sectors or segments of the market are riskier than others. Let's take a balanced fund for example. By definition a balanced fund usually invests 60 percent of its portfolio in equities and the remaining 40 percent in bonds or income-producing securities. And any buying or selling has to consider that balance or ratio, thus the name balanced fund.

Since bonds are traditionally safer than equities, balanced funds are considered less risky. Let's repeat that another way: equities historically return more than bonds and that's why equities have what's called a risk premium. Remember, the greater the return the greater the risk.

During the fabulous bull market many so-called pundits, among them Jeremy Siegel, a Wharton finance professor and author of *Stocks for the Long Run*, loved propagating the idea that because it was a new era equities deserved a smaller risk premium. Inflation remained low, productivity and earnings high, just-in-time inventory was all the rage. Siegel was still saying such right up to the spring of 2000 when the fat lady finally burst into song. Less risky to what, you may ask? Well, less risky compared to a highflying, high-growth small capitalization fund that concentrates on finding very small but very fast growing firms. The presence of bonds in the portfolio (all things equal, which in the market they hardly ever are) serves to dampen volatility, something most new investors view as their worst nightmare. Volatility in the stock market is measured by something call beta. We warned you about terminology. Here's a definition of beta taken from *Wall Street Words* by David Scott.

beta *A mathematical measure of the sensitivity of rates of return on a portfolio or given stock compared with rates of return on the market as a whole. A high beta (greater than 1.0) indicates moderate or high price volatility. A beta of 1.5 forecasts a 1.5% change in the return of the market. High beta stocks are best to own in a strong bull market but worst to own in a bear market.*

Now you didn't think there could be a beta without an alpha. Simply put, as we've already previously noted, alpha is about excess return, supposedly the benefit professional managements add to the value of your investments.

alpha *The mathematical estimate of the return on a security when the return on the market as a whole is zero.*

So follow this. An alpha of 1 means the stock has, on average, beaten the market by 1 percent per month, so if the market is up 10 percent in eight months, that stock should be up 18 percent. That's the so-called value added, as noted, of professional management.

Like the line in the Beetle's classic about "All we're saying is give peace a chance," all beta does is give investors a benchmark to compare a stock or mutual fund against. It's like one of those speedometer checks you occasionally see out on the highway. The S&P 500 Index has a beta of 1.0. So if you purchase a stock with a beta of 3.0, your stock is three times as volatile as the general market. That means it could go up in value in a bull market faster than the general market, but it also means the reverse is equally true. If you buy a mutual fund with a beta of, say, 0.5, your fund is not only less volatile than the general market but it will most likely under perform when the market is rising. It also means it will probably decline less in a falling market. Other than knowing about beta, it is not something investors need to pay much attention to. Numerous studies over the years question its real significance. Think of it as a speed limit sign and the odometer on your car. You need to have a benchmark as to how fast you are going and how fast the law legally allows. When it comes to small growth stocks, there is no law or speed limit; they can spend a lot of time on the autobahn. You can get a sense of that without looking for a speed limit sign and checking your odometer every five minutes. Not all traffic travels at the posted speed limit and neither do all stocks.

Most writers about the market or mutual funds give readers a list of fund families. We are not most writers. Look through the financial pages of your daily newspaper or go online and look up funds and you'll find lots of mutual fund families. If anything that is nearly all that remains today, larger mutual fund organizations that offer whole gaggles of funds to choose from. It is about what economists call economies of scale. To be cost efficient, the smaller or mom and pop firms have to attract gobs of capital. Attracting capital costs money. There are also fund-rating agencies like Morningstar, Value Line and Lipper that track fund performance and rate the various funds. And "Forbes" magazine every August puts out an issue devoted to fund performance that's worth a gander or two. If you're going to invest in mutual funds you should be apprised of these fund-rating firms, but not married to them. You can get lots of information, all you'll want in fact, about mutual funds online.

Now it's almost impossible to talk about mutual funds and the recent dark clouds wafting over the industry without mentioning fees. Yes, there are fees and that includes such linguistic legerdemain as load and no-load funds. If nature doesn't allow free lunches, what makes you believe that an industry that thrives on revenue, funds under management, would? The mutual fund industry is about profit and that profit can come from two sources—capital gains and fees. They receive the former if they pick stocks that prove winners; they pocket the latter either way. In other words, they get paid whether they are successful or not, nice duty if one can get it. It's a gig any politician worthy of the name readily appreciates.

There are scores of mutual funds that have been in business for scores of years that would put a new meaning to the term mediocre. That poses the question, if their performance is so average, why do investors stay the course? The answer, in our judgment, puts the lie to all those efficient market theorists, not to mention all those politicians who would legislatively mandate rational behavior; lots of folks for whatever reasons, and the reasons are legion, shun rationality. It comes with the right to life, happiness and the pursuit of liberty. In a semi-free nation such as America, Americans are still free for the nonce to do dumb things like daily wolf down their sustenance at fast-food joints or suck on cancer sticks or re-elect politicians who unabashedly dole out the swine.

From our viewpoint, the greatest thing about the Constitution of these United States is not freedom of assembly, freedom of worship or freedom of speech. It's the implied right to be irrational and behave irrationally. In other words, you have the right to be stupid, to do stupid things and, though probably not for long, to remain stupid. You still (for how much longer no one knows) have the right to be ignorant and to do ignorant stuff. And since ignorance is no excuse in the eyes of the law, think about what will happen to all those court fees and Internal Revenue penalties if ignorance is outlawed. In fact, one could make a strong case that if ignorance is proscribed, all meaningful, long-term learning will stop. For it turns out that life's biggest, most memorable lessons are usually garnered from our failures not our successes. Banish that right and the so-called wonderful experiment that began in 1776 really is history.

As an investor in mutual funds you need to be aware; fees matter. And there are all types from 12b-1, fees many mutual funds charge for so-called advertising and marketing, to management fees to up front or rear end exit fees called loads. If a fund charges you 1.75 percent management fees and you can find another similar fund that provides a similar performance for, say, a 0.75 percent management fee, you don't have to be a student of higher mathematics to figure out which one will best serve your purpose over the long haul. And that brings up another critical point. If you don't know what you're purpose is you'd better quickly find out. Mutual funds are not in business to voluntarily remit your investment because you don't know that you shouldn't be in a sector fund because it may prove unpalatable to your risk-level taste buds. Most folks don't know if they like a particular food until they try it. And most investors don't know what their risk tolerance is until they have been under the rifle. That usually means they have lost a few bucks. It use to be that a word to the discerning was sufficient, but that was pre-government bureaucrats and their interminable forms.

Cutting through the fascia and fat, here are some other things you need to be aware of about mutual funds. No, this is not some twisted form of the old exercise about kicking an industry when it's down. It's a point of information for you; make of it what you will. What was one of the primary criticisms about tobacco? Hook customers when they are young, get them addicted early, and you'll enjoy a steady stream of cash flow for years. That's pretty much what they're saying today about the fast food folks and the PC swelter that's erupted over portion sizes. How's that any different from mutual funds and many in the mutual fund industry preaching the long-term, buy-and-hold gospel? For tobacco and fast food companies it is cash flow, for mutual funds it's about management fees, the steadier the better.

Shakespeare warned about the Ides of March. Mutual fund investors need to be leery of advertising, especially the kind that touts the latest winners or the best funds. Some of the better funds hardly ever advertise. I had a friend who burned through thousands looking for his lifetime soul mate only to back into her patrol car with his new Humvee early one morning at the corner Crispy Cream. He still goes around bragging about what a deal he got for the price of that ticket. We've already warned about fees and portfolio turnover; both can run up costs.

When is the last time you saw were 100 percent was the average for anything? Well, that's the average portfolio turnover rate for mutual funds, 100 percent. Some funds with higher costs are really closet index funds. That means you're probably paying more than you should be for an index fund. Though costs vary, index funds are among the cheapest in the industry. Do you wolf down your own vittles? Well, most of the mutual funds on Eliot Spitzer's persona non-gratis list didn't. Look for funds where management has kicked in some of their own hard-to-come by juice. It's not foolproof, nothing is. But at least they have more at stake than the ordinary mutual fund manager.

Here is a brief summary of mutual fund definitions: Read them and reap!

MUTUAL FUND: an investment company that invests its shareholders' money in a portfolio of securities.

LOAD FUND: a mutual fund that charges a commission when shares are bought. Also call a front-end load fund.

NO-LOAD: a mutual fund that does not charge a commission when shares are bought. (Note: that doesn't mean no-load funds don't have fees.)

LOW-LOAD: a mutual fund that charges a small commission (2% to 3%) when shares are purchased.

BACK-END LOAD: a commission gets charged when shares are sold.

12(b)-1 FEE: a fee the fund charges to cover advertising and marketing or other operating costs, in some cases as much as 1% of net assets.

POOLED FUNDS: a process where investors buy a diversified portfolio of securities for the collective benefit of individual investors.

CLOSED-END FUND: an investment company that is traded on an exchange and offers a fixed number of outstanding shares as opposed to mutual funds which do not trade on an exchange and can offer an unlimited number of shares.

UNIT INVESTMENT TRUST: a type of mutual fund in that the trust sponsors pool investors' money to purchase a fixed, unmanaged portfolio of securities and then offer units of ownership to individual investors. Usually the securities are of the fixed type, like municipal bonds, and remained fixed without any active trading until the trusts expire. One caveat, these trusts can have higher costs with load running in the 2% to 3%range and 1% to 2% in annual fees.

Though most of these have been mentioned in the text, if might be good to briefly review the various types of funds. This list is hardly exhaustive, however.

GROWTH FUND: a mutual fund that invests in a portfolio of stocks with the primary goal of providing long-term capital gains and appreciation or growth.

AGGRESSIVE GROWTH: the term speaks for itself in that aggressive growth funds are speculative and they seek big profits from capital gains.

EQUITY INCOME: a fund that emphasizes current income with an emphasis on capital preservation and invests primarily in income-producing or high-yielding securities.

BALANCE: a fund that seeks a balanced return from both capital gains and current income. The fund usually has a balanced mix of equities and bonds.

BOND FUND: a fund that seeks income from investing in a varied portfolio of bonds with various grades that provides as their primary objective income to shareholders.

VALUE FUND: a fund that seeks equities that are undervalued and offer future gains. These equities are often overlooked or out-of-favor stocks that usually have low p/e ratios and high dividends

GROWTH AND INCOME: these funds differ from equity-income funds in that these funds seek long-term capital gains first and income second.

INDEX FUND: a mutual fund that buys and holds a portfolio of stocks or bonds that reflects or is equivalent to those in a specific market index. Though there are numerous others, the most common one is the S&P 500 Index.

MONEY MARKET FUND: a mutual fund that pools investors' money and invest in short-term money market instruments.

SECTOR FUND: a mutual find that invests in a portfolio of a specific sector of the economy like energy or technology or defense.

SOCIALLY RESONSIBLE FUND: a mutual fund that invest in a portfolio of stock whose underlying company does not do business in industries that can cause personal of environmental harm like tobacco or pollution or defense.

INTERNATIONAL FUND: a mutual fun that invests mostly in foreign securities. Note some make a distinction between international and global funds.

ASSET ALLOCATION FUND: in simple terms this is a mutual fund that seeks the right assets at the right time, emphasizing diversification and consistency rather that hitting homeruns.

It is safe to conclude that this chapter has barely skimmed the surface when it comes to mutual funds. But it's a launching point. That old Chinese saying about a long journey beginning when you put that first foot in front of the other applies to the world of investing more so than you'll ever imagine. Though caveat emptor in today's PC world has become about as politically incorrect as homophobia, just remember this; investing has nothing to do with sighs and kisses; it has everything to do with your time, your money and your future.

CHAPTER SEVEN

If you think education is expensive, try ignorance.

Bumper Sticker

ETFs

There is a new kid in town. His name is ETFs, exchange traded funds. And they could turn out to be a bigger nightmare for the mutual fund industry than insider trading, questionable fees, excessive portfolio turnover and any other as yet undiscovered hanky panky. It is doubtful but they could even someday cause the Eliot Spitzers of the universe to seek honest employment. On the other hand, some people view honest employment as about attractive as a case of SARS.

Hybrids are rampant in nature. And the investing world is not much different. Bonds have convertible bonds, equities convertible preferred stocks and options have their puts and calls which can be either traded or exercised, in a way a hybrid feature in their own right. Part index fund, part stock, ETFs are the latest hybrids available to retail investors. And they make a lot of sense. Here's why.

Exchange trade funds put the in-control button back in the hands of individual investors. No more do they have to worry about willy-nilly board directors who arbitrarily vote themselves pay hikes. And besides being simple to understand, they trade just like stocks do, throughout the day which gives the investor at least three immediate advantages: you don't have to wait, as mentioned, until closing to get a quote if you're buying or selling; fees are low and they offer almost as many choices as an old-time cafeteria.

You'll need a broker, online or otherwise, to buy and sell, but that's hardly a sound reason for avoiding them. And you can do just about anything you want; buy ETFs that mimic specific indexes; concentrate in one sector or country or hedge, to name a few. Say you want to play the S&P 500 index, you can. Or maybe you want to get some money invested outside the U.S. like MSCI-EAFE, the Morgan Stanley index of stocks for trading in Europe, Australia and the Far East. Or maybe you want to load up on a particular sector, like basic materials, you definitely can. In fact, from biotech to energy to transportation, there is an ETF. You like technology, there are currently 16 technology ETFs to choose from. And there are ETFs for real estate and bonds, too. Like their equity brethren, bond ETFs are hybrids also, part index, part bonds. And there are corporate bond and Treasury bond ETFs, so if you recall the term and what it means, pick your own duration. Or maybe you want some exposure to the health care sector, but you want to avoid the hassle of picking individual securities in that industry; there is a health care ETF. An ETF to trade gold has also been approved by the SEC, and is now trading. And you can bet there will be more, so you can buy and sell gold ETFs to hedge inflation should you so choose.

Last count there was more than 100 ETFs now trading. And besides flexibility, ETFs offer tax efficiency not always available with mutual funds due to the high portfolio turnover many mutual funds have chasing those slippery profits or capital gains. They can be bought on margin and shorted, even on a downtick, something that has been prohibited with common stocks since the 1930s when those omniscient regulators decided the 1929 crash was caused by short sellers and changed the rules. (Now don't get yourself puffed up like a big ball of cotton candy here. Selling short is a way to make money when a stock or bond or whatever goes down in value. It's a concept many new investors find difficult to understand, but it is quite common.) Here's a brief list of some of the more popular ETFs. If you want more information, go to Amex.com and click on, what else, ETFs. And just a reminder, remember back in the chapter on bonds we discussed passive-aggressive investing. Well, ETFs can certainly be used to invest either passively or aggressively or, if you like to hedge, both.

AMEX Exchange Traded Funds (ETFs)

Broad-Based Indexes	Symbol
DIAMONDS®	DIA
FORTUNE 500 Index Tracking Stock®	FFF
MidCap SPDRS™	MDY
NASDAQ -100 Index Tracking Stock	QQQ
SPDRS˙ (Standard & Poor's Depositary Receipts)	SPY
Vanguard Extended Market VIPERS	VXF
Vanguard Total Stock Market VIPERS	VTI
iShares Dow Jones U.S. Total Market Index Fund	IYY
iShares Russell 1000 Growth Index Fund	IWF
iShares Russell 1000 Index Fund	IWB
iShares Russell 1000 Value Index Fund	IWD
iShares Russell 2000 Growth Index Fund	IWO
iShares Russell 2000 Index Fund	IWM
iShares Russell 2000 Value Index Fund	IWN
iShares Russell 3000 Growth Index Fund	IWZ
iShares Russell 3000 Index Fund	IWV
iShares Russell 3000 Value Index Fund	IWW
iShares Russel MidCap Growth Index Fund	IWP
iShares Russel MidCap Index Fund	IWR

iShares Russel MidCap Value Index Fund	IWS
iShares S&P 500 Index Fund	IVV
iShares S&P 500/BARRA Growth Index Fund	IVW
iShares S&P 500/BARRA Value Index Fund	IVE
iShares S&P MidCap 400 Index Fund	IJH
iShares S&P MidCap 400/BARRA Growth Index Fund	IJK
iShares S&P MidCap 400/BARRA Value Index Fund	IJJ
iShares S&P SmallCap 600 Index Fund	IJR
iShares S&P SmallCap 600/BARRA Growth Index Fund	IJT
iShares S&P SmallCap 600/BARRA Value Index Fund	IJS
streetTRACKS Dow Jones U.S. Global Titans Index Fund	DGT
streetTRACKS Dow Jones U.S. Large Cap Growth Index Fund	ELG
streetTRACKS Dow Jones U.S. Large Cap Value Index Fund	ELV
streetTRACKS Dow Jones U.S. Small Cap Growth Index Fund	DSG
streetTRACKS Dow Jones U.S. Small Cap Value Index Fund	DSV

Industry Sector	Symbol
FORTUNE e-50™ Index Tracking Stock	FEF
Select Sector SPDR - Basic Industries	XLB
Select Sector SPDR - Consumer Services	XLV
Select Sector SPDR - Consumer Staples	XLP
Select Sector SPDR - Cyclical/Transportation	XLY
Select Sector SPDR - Energy	XLE

Select Sector SPDR - Financial	XLF
Select Sector SPDR - Industrial	XLI
Select Sector SPDR - Technology	XLK
Select Sector SPDR - Utilities	XLU
iShares Cohen & Steers Realty Majors Index Fund	ICF
iShares Dow Jones U.S. Basic Materials Sector Index Fund	IYM
iShares Dow Jones U.S. Chemical Index Fund	IYD
iShares Dow Jones U.S. Consumer Cyclical Sector Index Fund	IYC
iShares Dow Jones U.S. Consumer Non-Cyclical Sector Index Fund	IYK
iShares Dow Jones U.S. Energy Sector Index Fund	IYE
iShares Dow Jones U.S. Financial Sector Index Fund	IYF
iShares Dow Jones U.S. Financial Services Index Fund	IYG
iShares Dow Jones U.S. Healthcare Sector Index Fund	IYH
iShares Dow Jones U.S. Industrial Sector Index Fund	IYJ
iShares Dow Jones U.S. Internet Index Fund	IYV
iShares Dow Jones U.S. Real Estate Index Fund	IYR
iShares Dow Jones U.S. Technology Sector Index Fund	IYW
iShares Dow Jones U.S. Telecommunications Sector Index Fund	IYZ
iShares Dow Jones U.S. Utilities Sector Index Fund	IDU
iShares Goldman Sachs Natural Resources Index Fund	IGE
iShares Goldman Sachs Networking Index Fund	IGN
iShares Goldman Sachs Semiconductor Index Fund	IGW
iShares Goldman Sachs Software Index Fund	IGV

iShares Goldman Sachs Technology Index Fund	IGM
iShares NASDAQ Biotechnology Index Fund	IBB
iShares S&P Global Energy Index Fund	IXC
iShares S&P Global Financials Index Fund	IXG
iShares S&P Global Healthcare Index Fund	IXJ
iShares S&P Global Information Technology Index Fund	IXN
iShares S&P Global Telecommunications Index Fund	IXP
streetTRACKS Morgan Stanley High Tech 35 Index Fund	MTK
streetTRACKS Morgan Stanley Internet Index Fund	MII
streetTRACKS Wilshire REIT Index Fund	RWR

International Indexes .... Symbol

iShares MSCI - Australia

Trading Symbol	EWA
I.O.P.V (Indicative Optimized Portfolio Value)	WBJ
Shares Outstanding	QAW

iShares MSCI - Austria

Trading Symbol	EWO
I.O.P.V (Indicative Optimized Portfolio Value)	INY
Shares Outstanding	QAU

iShares MSCI - Belgium

Trading Symbol	EWK
I.O.P.V (Indicative Optimized Portfolio Value)	INK

Shares Outstanding	BES

iShares MSCI - Brazil

Trading Symbol	EWZ
I.O.P.V (Indicative Optimized Portfolio Value)	WWC
Shares Outstanding	SKH

iShares MSCI - Canada

Trading Symbol	EWC
I.O.P.V (Indicative Optimized Portfolio Value)	WPB
Shares Outstanding	QCN

iShares MSCI - EAFE

Trading Symbol	EFA
I.O.P.V (Indicative Optimized Portfolio Value)	EFV
Shares Outstanding	EFV.SO

iShares MSCI - EMU

(European Monetary Union)

Trading Symbol	EZU
I.O.P.V (Indicative Optimized Portfolio Value)	WWE
Shares Outstanding	SJE

iShares MSCI - France

Trading Symbol	EWQ
I.O.P.V (Indicative Optimized Portfolio Value)	WBF
Shares Outstanding	SXF

iShares MSCI - Germany

| Trading Symbol | EWG |

I.O.P.V (Indicative Optimized Portfolio Value) — WDG

Shares Outstanding — QGE

iShares MSCI - Hong Kong

Trading Symbol — EWH

I.O.P.V (Indicative Optimized Portfolio Value) — INH

Shares Outstanding — SHK

iShares MSCI - Italy

Trading Symbol — EWI

I.O.P.V (Indicative Optimized Portfolio Value) — INE

Shares Outstanding — SIT

iShares MSCI - Japan

Trading Symbol — EWJ

I.O.P.V (Indicative Optimized Portfolio Value) — INJ

Shares Outstanding — SJA

iShares MSCI - Malaysia

Trading Symbol — EWM

I.O.P.V (Indicative Optimized Portfolio Value) — INM

Shares Outstanding — SMY

iShares MSCI - Mexico

Trading Symbol — EWW

I.O.P.V (Indicative Optimized Portfolio Value) — INW

Shares Outstanding	QMX

iShares MSCI - Netherlands

Trading Symbol	EWN
I.O.P.V (Indicative Optimized Portfolio Value)	INN
Shares Outstanding	NTS

iShares MSCI - Pacific Ex-Japan

Trading Symbol	EPP
I.O.P.V (Indicative Optimized Portfolio Value)	EPK
Shares Outstanding	EPK.SO

iShares MSCI - Singapore

Trading Symbol	EWS
I.O.P.V (Indicative Optimized Portfolio Value)	INR
Shares Outstanding	QSG

iShares MSCI - South Korea

Trading Symbol	EWY
I.O.P.V (Indicative Optimized Portfolio Value)	WWK
Shares Outstanding	

iShares MSCI - Spain

Trading Symbol	EWP
I.O.P.V (Indicative Optimized Portfolio Value)	INP
Shares Outstanding	QSN

iShares MSCI - Sweden

Trading Symbol	EWD

I.O.P.V (Indicative Optimized Portfolio Value)	WBQ
Shares Outstanding	SWE

iShares MSCI - Switzerland

Trading Symbol	EWL
I.O.P.V (Indicative Optimized Portfolio Value)	INL
Shares Outstanding	QSW

iShares MSCI - Taiwan

Trading Symbol	EWT
I.O.P.V (Indicative Optimized Portfolio Value)	WWM
Shares Outstanding	SJF

iShares MSCI - United Kingdom

Trading Symbol	EWU
I.O.P.V (Indicative Optimized Portfolio Value)	INU
Shares Outstanding	UKS

iShares S&P Europe 350

Trading Symbol	IEV
I.O.P.V (Indicative Optimized Portfolio Value)	NLG
Shares Outstanding	OBD

iShares S&P Latin America 40 Index Fund

Trading Symbol	ILF
I.O.P.V (Indicative Optimized Portfolio Value)	NIH
Shares Outstanding	NIH.SO

iShares S&P/TOPIX 150 Index Fund

Trading Symbol	ITF
I.O.P.V (Indicative Optimized Portfolio Value)	NIT
Shares Outstanding	NIT.SO

iShares S&P/TSE 60 Index Fund

Trading Symbol	IKC
I.O.P.V (Indicative Optimized Portfolio Value)	NLJ
Shares Outstanding	OCD
FRESCO DJ japan Titans 100	FJD

CHAPTER EIGHT

The truth has a horrible sweat to survive in this world, but a piece of nonsense, however absurd on its face, always seems to prosper.

H.L. Mencken

MARKET MYTHS

Market myths are like well-intentioned friends who will get you killed in combat or who inform you, while inhaling a thick cloud of gray smoke, that their grandmother lived to be 98, inhaling two packs of cigarettes before breakfast everyday and a couple of Cuban cigars on Saturday and Sunday. (Besides longevity, at least the old gal had good taste!) Market timing is one of the more popular ones. Usually, it's stated by the pundits like this: nobody can time the market. Others hedge by seeking the safer ground of qualification, spouting no one can "consistently" time the market. The pundits love to slip in a properly placed adverb or adjective. Translation: because I can't neither can you nor anybody else and therefore you shouldn't try.

This is one of those myths that it is almost too much fun to demystify or is that, should we say, demythify. New York Attorney General Eliot Spitzer apparently believes someone was profitably timing the market; otherwise he has no case for suing all those mutual fund companies. And speaking of mutual fund firms, why do you think most of them prohibit investors (shareholders, that is) from making more than four or five trades a year, imposing heavy fees for those who exceed the allowed number? We all know the excuse they cite, it disrupts the portfolio, increases paper work and costs, and is unfair to long-term shareholders. It is also terribly unfair to and terribly draining on management fees.

Then there are all those traders on the commodity and futures floor trading everyday, many successful, many making millions of dollars annually. Down there things get marked to market daily, meaning you're either profitable or you find other work. Read both volumes of Jack Schwager's *Market Wizards Interviews with Top Traders* if you want to learn about people who time the market successfully. True they are all professionals, but that's how you know many of these pundits are up to their ear lobes in it: They love to use qualifications, but only when those qualifiers suit their point of view. There are roughly six billion folks on planet earth. (We know this because we trudged through Al Gore's *Earth in the Balance*.) To disprove any theory all you need is one exception. The odds against not finding just one out of six billion who can successfully do something, anything, are astronomical. That's a statistical number even economists should appreciate. Nobody could supposedly run a sub-four minute mile until one day a fellow named Roger Banister showed up. They have been running sub-four minute miles ever since. Everybody? No, not everybody, but enough to make it commonplace.

For those who recall their history of the Spanish American War, "Remember the Maine" was a popular slogan. Now the anti-timing pundits will cite the work of Nobel prize-winning economist William Sharpe, the founder of Modern Portfolio Theory. Simply stated (not that Nobel prize-winning economists ever stated anything simply), Sharpe's work centered on a statistical method for minimizing risk while maximizing returns.

What the study showed was an investor who tries to time the market needs to be correct about three of every four times versus the old tortoise technique of buying and holding. Seventy five percent correct in anything is a daunting figure. Recall those baseball players who make mini-fortunes being correct with less than half that number. Our response is: Remember Long-Term Capital Management, the hedge fund that in the late 1990s nearly went belly-up until Alan Greenspan and his central banking monetary vaqueros rode to its rescue. Long-

Term Capital Management had not one but two Nobel prize-winning economists working their statistical magic to guide the fund. Some might suggest the LTCM pratfall further proves you can't time the market. To us the only thing it proves is trust Nobel prize-winning economists at your own peril.

Diversification is another term you'll hear much about. Some refer to it as "deworsification." It is one of those good-sounding half-truths similar to the many most of us learned while incarcerated during our youth in those ivy-covered structures called college campuses. They sound correct and, after all, usually come from on high. Super investor Warren Buffet's portfolio is pretty concentrated. Sure he owns lots of different companies, but they meet quite limited criteria. One of the themes they share is they are all pretty much "old economy" stocks. Check it out. Diversification is the inverse of putting all your eggs in one basket, but no less risky. It's the Good House keeping stamp of investment mediocrity. As some have adroitly noted diversification is the epitome of not knowing what the hell you're doing. You can't decide on rolls or muffins or bagels for dinner, so you get three dozen of each.

In his classic *The Battle for Investment Survival*, Gerald Loeb wrote: "Diversification is a necessity for the beginner. On the other hand, the really great fortunes were made by concentration." Focus on that term concentration. Did Bill Gates amass his fortune by dabbling in selling used cars or running restaurants? And even old Warren Buffett famously centered his efforts on non-technology companies, a kind of concentration in itself.

These same pundits will shout that diversification and strategic, whatever the hell that is, asset allocation minimizes volatility. Now follow this illogical premise to its illogical conclusion. You purchase a stock because you're looking for some action, some movement, some volatility; (There, we said it!); in this case, upside. If you were short, you'd welcome downside volatility. Do you want to purchase a stock and watch it just mope around like a bowl of corn flakes that's been in the refrigerator for two days. Unless you're a spread trader you don't. You should note how volatility for many of these pundits means only downside risk. Think about your life, ever had any volatility in it? Some of it has obviously been bad and some of it hasn't been all that bad at all. Now imagine a volatility-free existence. Getting excited yet?

Volatility is hardly your enemy, especially if you're trading options. But that's another topic for another time. You'll never have all the information you need to make a decision. "If you did," as someone wisely stated, "it would be a foregone conclusion, not a decision." And that's exactly what those who tout things like strategic asset allocation, or whatever they choose to name it this month, are doing; they're trying to eliminate volatility from something that is inherently volatile, markets. They seek to ensure a guarantee to something that's never been guaranteed. If you're having trouble following the bouncing ball here, think life. And should they prove successful, it would not and could not be the same. Just suppose we were able through some quirk of science, cloning should come to mind, to remove the human from human being. Would the species still be the same? That is one of the sure fire ways you can pick out true-blue bureaucrats; they want to take the fat out of the food and still call it food. The anti-volatility bunch is just another branch from the same phylum as the zero-risk PC crowd.

And what is this asset allocation, strategic or otherwise, these pundits are constantly screaming about? Defined simply, it means spreading your investments across different types of investments, say, stocks, bonds, real estate, commodities; whereas diversification simply means buying more than one security in each investment type. This is another one of those it-sounds-great deals, not too different from what people frequently claim they do versus what they actually do. When the stock market took off in August 1982 and, with few exceptions hardly looked in the rear view mirror, very few retail investors were even in the market. Commodities at the same time were also taking off, but in a totally different direction, falling into a 20-year downward funk during which time they hardly bothered to look up. You need to note this because many pundits, to justify their claims, like to print charts like the one here.

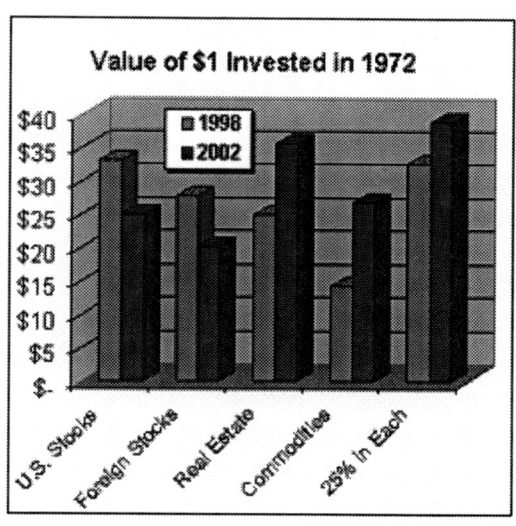

This chart shows that had you invested $1 dollar in 1972 in each of the 4 categories (U.S. Stocks, Foreign Stocks, Real Estate, Commodities) instead of concentrating your money in just a select one or two, 30 years later you'd be lighting up the big cigar. Not so fast. This is the type of simple-minded, linear thinking that can be detrimental to your wealth. In 1973-74 a mother-of-all bear markets arrived and 10 years later most investors were still nursing their wounds. And those who did conjure up the courage, and some capital, to get back in found themselves ambushed again in the crash of 1987. In fact, nearly all recent research shows that the hordes of retail investors didn't pile into the stock market until the mid-to-late 1990s, not too far from the top.

Though real estate and commodity prices went on a tear owing to inflation in the 1970s, it was next to impossible for the so-called average guy (with perhaps the exception of sauntering into a coin shop to buy a Kuggerand or pick up a bag or two of old silver coins) to play commodities in those days. And buying real estate wasn't much easier. By the late '70s and early '80s, with inflation and mortgage rates hovering near 15 percent, few could even qualify to buy a home or anything else for that matter.

But just suppose you were shrewd enough to try the surrogate route to real estate fame and fortune by buying REITs on one of the stock exchanges. The idea behind REITs gained popularity in the 1960s; it was the new kid in town and for a while enjoyed a rousing welcome. In the 1973-74 bear market, however, REITs got hammered, suffering their worse downturn ever. As John Dennis Brown states in his excellent book *Panic Profits*: "...nearly 300 stocks lost more than 50 percent of their value, led by REITs and mortgage companies."

And then there is the little matter of psychology or what's now called Behavioral Finance. Between fear and greed, research reveals fear is the far greater motivator of the two. So not only is it unrealistic but down right misleading to suggest that ordinary investors, assuming they could have even played these stormy markets, would have stayed with the ship for the entire 30-year period. But there is even another psychological fact at work here. Once the big bull market gained its full stride, financial assets became the de jour dish of the period. The higher they climbed, the more money investors poured into them and the more financial advisors touted their prowess. It became a self-feeding financial frenzy.

So given that scenario what investor, average or otherwise, would have consciously left 25 percent of her funds in an asset that was getting smoked in comparison. And for that matter how do you think a financial advisor's advice to leave 25 percent of your funds stashed in commodities during the greatest run-up in financial assets in history would have been received? The truth is asset allocation during much of the 1980s and all of the 1990s was about financial assets. And greed and fear are the two main reasons: greed to make it while it's there to be made and fear of being left out.

And here is one more example to consider when you come across those pundits who like to extrapolate the future from the past, carefully selecting the correct graphs and charts to buttress their point. Now 30-year Treasury bonds didn't exist until the 1970s and they were retired during Clinton's last term. (Note: in 2005 the Bush administration decided to re-issue the 30-Treasury bond.). So we have to use what's called a synthetic here, but it doesn't matter. If you allocated 20 percent of your assets to 30-year T-bonds in 1946 and held on for dear life until 1981, you would have seen 83 percent of your principle disappear.

If anything the great bull market of the 1990s with its mania for capital gains worked against assets being allocated to any other class than financial assets. Like every bull market, it made a mockery of the old saying about a bird in hand, dividends or taking some profits off the table, being worth two in the bush. It was all about upcoming-yet-to-be-realized capital gains few were willing to risk missing out on. So the next time you read one of those cute little "It's Really Easy to Do!" investing articles on the Internet or in some proletariat magazine, remember to check out the history books.

And remember too many of these so-called financial journalists actually missed their calling. They should have forgone journalism and gone into mining, data mining. Simply stated, that's where you dig up the data that will support your premise conveniently ignoring any contrary data. You will hear and see many stories, often put out by insurance companies selling annuities and mutual funds, about holding equities for any 20-year period has proved profitable. Well, yes and no. In early 2006 the London School of Economics produced a 100-year study showing in many stock markets around the globe investors failed to get even over periods as long as 50-years. In fact, much of the distortion about investors getting even earlier came from factoring in U.S. stock market data.

So there might be a whiff of warning here in the current craze, not unlike the Internet bubble years, of retail investors sending hordes of their money into emerging markets around the globe.

CHAPTER NINE

Affairs are easier of entrance than exit; and it is but common prudence to see our way out before we venture in.

Aesop

ANNUITIES

Somehow one has to believe George Dubya's advisors never read old Aesop. For some reason lots of folks, many of them quite sophisticated, have difficulty grasping the concept of annuities. So let's go back to some basic English—like plain old nouns and verbs. A noun, you'll recall, is defined as a person, place or thing. With verbs it's mostly about action or existence. Sure there are such goodies as transitive and intransitive verbs, but that's perhaps another manual. (We knew you really wanted to know, so here it is: Transitive verbs require direct objects to complete their meaning. Intransitive verbs don't. Could it be any simpler?)

An annuity is an insurance contract sold by an insurance company. Essentially, there are two types of annuities, variable and fixed. The first, variable, falls under the scrutiny of the Security and Exchange Commission because it's classified as a security, like stocks and bonds. Fixed annuities are not considered securities because fixed annuities are governed by the state insurance commissions. So here's a subtle but important difference. To sell variable annuities one must possess a valid securities' license as in Series Six or Seven. Not the case with fixed annuities. One need only possess an insurance license to hawk them and over the years there's been much hawking.

Now back to some more basic English. One of the age-old ploys of journalists and Madison Avenue types (Remember these two groups are responsible for most of the world's ills!) is to take any poor, puny, unsuspecting noun and turn it into a verb by adding -ize to the end. Take the original noun *verb* and convert it into verbalize and you're starting to get it. It can be an endless and somewhat ornery game: Sermon to sermonize, final to finalize, capital to capitalize, vital to vitalize, to revitalize (which is what many folks were hoping the stock market would do anytime now since the 2000 meltdown started.). Anyway, we told you it was ongoing. People who overeat are known to pork out. So you might say that they get porked. And you'll remember that Yale University conservative Constitutional law scholar Robert Bork got borked when the Senate failed to confirm his nomination to the United States Supreme Court a few years ago. Laugh not. Nearly every judge now who fails to get nominated to a higher court is referred to in the media as having been borked. It's a term that's found its place in the American lexicon.

So what does all this have to do with annuities? Just this: annuity is a noun and so is the person, or annuitant, who purchases one. He or she is the owner. And when the annuitant finally wants to cash in her annuity at the end of the contract, assuming that person does, she annuitizes the darn thing. How much more simple can it be than that? And that gets us to just what kinds or types of annuities exist and how they can be annuitized. But here's a little sidebar: fewer than 2 percent of annuity owners ever annuitize.

Before we do, however, remember this. Annuities are a lot like my neighbor who shocked the neighborhood one day when he painted his house purple and the front door bright red, not for everyone: Feng Shui at work in the old neighborhood. You'll recall that Feng Shui was big in Silicon Valley during the dot.com mania. Much like the new paradigm, Feng Shui would provide a new harmony to the new-age productivity Federal Reserve Chairman Alan Greenspan liked to rave about. Feng Shui and annuities share one commonality: around our office we refer to both as NFE's, not for everyone. So plowing through this chapter will help you decide if annuities are for you or your favorite uncle or your grandparents or your loveable pet. (Don't get crazy on me. People sometimes use annuities in their estate planning to make sure Hondo gets his lamb and rice vittles.)

We're talking language here. Technology, law, medicine and sports all have their own language. Even those good old boys (and girls) in auto racing have a special vocabulary. So it shouldn't surprise you that the world of investing, and that includes insurance, has its own vernacular. We left out nursing because you already understand that language. (See. We know from which side our manual reads best.)

Annuities are essentially an insurance product because variable or fixed, they have an insurance component. Though some mutual fund companies offer annuities, annuities are sold mostly by insurance companies. In short, annuities are a contract between the purchaser and the insurance company. So you're starting to get the picture. And along the way you'll gain a better understanding of our quote from Aesop. Recently, *Barron's*, the weekly business journal that's been around since Moses carted the tablets down, decided to stop listing annuities in the magazine's statistical section. There's no hidden meaning here, just a point of information.

If diseases have certain characteristics, what are the characteristics of annuities? For a while there I didn't think you'd ever ask. You already know an annuity is an investment you make through an insurance company. It's a contract. All contracts, in order to be such, have what attorneys call consideration. One party gets something and so does the other party. You decide to sell me your car for $1,800. I get your car and you get the cash. That's consideration. (By the way, did I get a good deal on your car?) In the case of an annuity the insurance company gets your money and you get certain assurances from the insurance company, things like a guaranteed rate of return or tax deferred growth, or a death benefit or all of the above, to mention just a few.

Annuities can be summarized in three ways: how is the money invested (fixed or variable); deferred or immediate, in this case we're talking about income; or whether the annuity is flexible or what's called single premium. Let's take first things first, as they say. The money can be invested at a fixed rate, similar to certificates of deposit sold by banks. The insurance company guarantees the annuitant, or contract owner, see I told you you'd catch on, a certain rate of return for a certain period of time. Like most other things in life, the longer the period the greater the rate of interest promised. So with a fixed-rate annuity investors receive a set rate of return. With variable annuities you're really talking mutual funds because the investor gets a variety of portfolios to choose from, ranging from money market to bonds to aggressive growth funds, but there is no promised or guaranteed rate of return. In the variable annuity world these portfolios are called sub accounts and investors' shares are called units not shares. (You could say it's about how insurance companies set themselves apart or make things difficult. Heaven forbid that we all call them shares in the name of uniformity!) So if you buy stocks or a mutual fund, you get shares; if you purchase a variable annuity, you get units.

The annuitant decides how the money gets invested and he or she can make changes just about any time. Now there is a subtle point here between variable and fixed rate annuities you don't want to miss. With the fixed-rate annuity, the insurance company decides where the money gets invested. So the burden of investment is on the insurance company. With the variable annuity, on the other hand, the investor decides where the money gets invested (e.g., money market, bond or stock fund) so the burden of investing is on the annuitant or contract owner. Why is that important? Well, just suppose you purchased a new annuity right after the stock market topped out in March 2000 and chose an aggressive growth fund. Given where the market is today, you'd still be under water. If on the other hand, you'd selected a bond fund, what with the way interest rates declined between 2000 and 2003 after the market crashed, your performance would have been much more appetizing. (See those bad journalists don't have anything on us. We can do it too.)

A little digression is in order. An annuitant or contract owner (By now you know they are one in the same, though they don't have to be, so from here on I will save my breath and my fingers.) can choose between an immediate annuity or a deferred annuity. Now don't get flustered. An immediate annuity is a type of fixed-rate or variable wherein the annuitant starts collecting his or her money right away or within a definite time period like a month or three months or one year. Immediate annuities are for those who need income on a regular basis. A deferred annuity, easily the more popular of the two, allows the investment to grow and compound tax-deferred until some future date. When that date arrives, the annuitant can if he or she chooses annuitize his annuity. (I told you all this before!) In short, he or she calls up the insurance company and says" "Start sending me my money."

Now we have to talk about premiums. We don't really have to, but I am sure you'll want to know this, but before we do that here's a little review. A variable annuity has two phases—an accumulation phase and a payout phase. During the accumulation phase you, or the contract owner, make purchase payments. Those payments can be allocated according to your risk appetite. For example, you can design your own portfolio, allocating, say, 40 percent to a U. S. stock fund, 40 percent to a bond fund and 20 percent to an international stock fund. The options are not limitless, but then what in life is. Those funds will grow or decline in value according to the performance of each fund you choose. Make poor selections and you get the idea. As we said, with variable annuities the burden of investing rests on your shoulders. During this accumulation phase you can generally transfer from one investment option to another without incurring penalties or taxes on your income and capital gains, if you have any. That's the tax deferred part. Now listen up, that doesn't mean that the insurance company can't charge you transfer fees or exit fees or penalties. Some might, others might not. Learn right here and now—fees matter. So read the contract and ask questions. Questions are free, the contract might not be. In other words, you should view before you vault, read before you run, gander before you gallop, study before you sign. Is that clear enough?

Now you've been in the accumulation phase for years and it's time to move on to the payout. Under this phase you have some choices. Decisions, decisions, like the water in Coleridge's "Rhyme of the Ancient Mariner," are everywhere and not a single potable drop to be found. Help! Everyone it seems deplores decisions, but get in, sit down, buckle up and get use to it. It's called Life 101.

How do you want to take this money, in a steady stream of payments that run for a specified period like, say, 20 years certain or a lump sum? We told you life isn't easy; you work hard and then you have to make decisions. Suppose you reside in California, the world capitol for low-carbohydrate diet freaks, and as luck would have it you win the state lottery. You have two ways, after taxes, to take the lucre, lump sum or in equal payments over, say, 20 years. If you decide to take it all up front, is this not a classic example of choosing current wealth over future wealth? And just the opposite is also true. If you take the payment route, you're essentially deciding at least somewhat to forgo current wealth for future wealth. We told you: life is about decisions. And decisions, like higher oil prices, don't happen in a vacuum.

There are two types of premiums, flexible and single. If by now you don't comprehend single, shame on you. A lump sum is used to buy an annuity. No more payments are necessary. That's called a single premium annuity. So flexible must mean additional monies can be added at any time to the same annuity contract, right? You're getting so smart. Of the two, flexible premiums are the more common, especially with variable annuities. Flexible premiums with fixed-rate annuities are rare.

So now let's pull a Hollywood and cut to the chase. What are the advantages and disadvantages of purchasing annuities? Annuities have advantages not always available in other types of investments. The money can compound tax-deferred, just as it does in most retirement accounts like Keoghs, IRAs and such. Annuities for the most part avoid probate, a nasty, costly experience most investors, whether they realize it or not, will want their heirs to avoid. Incidentally, the term probate means "prove the will." And it's a legal process that takes place even if one dies without a will or intestate, to use the legal jargon.

Annuities can provide a guaranteed death benefit. We told you annuities were an insurance contract. A guaranteed death benefit, and here we're talking only variable annuities, means the beneficiary receives the greater of the principal or the value of the account on the date of the annuitant's demise. Now let's try to simply this. If you the owner of the variable annuity should die, your beneficiary(s) will receive one of the following (notice we didn't say both!): all the money in your account or some guaranteed minimum that the insurance company promised you when you signed on like all purchase payments minus any withdrawals you may have made. Most variable annuity contracts will allow the owner to take out 10 percent a year without any penalties, so if you had taken out 10 percent at some time that amount would be subtracted from what your heir(s) would receive.

Most annuities have a withdrawal option. The annuitant, or owner, can withdraw up to 10 percent of the value of the contract per year without any penalty or fee. Gee! I think we already noted that. Some tout professional management as another plus, though that's open to interpretation. Tax-free exchanges are another advantage if correctly used. These tax-free exchanges are often called 1035s, a kind of roll over that skips the taxman. (Don't worry the tax collector, or as many refer to him, the low man, will find a way to get his share.)

Once again, here's what you need to know about: surrender charges. Surrender charges are to annuities like mustard is to hotdogs. Typically, when you purchase an annuity the contract has surrender charges that decrease each year over a certain period until they reach zero. Say you buy an annuity with a seven-year surrender period. The surrender charges may be 10 percent in years one through three and diminish to zero over the next four years. So if you try to exit or surrender the annuity in the first seven years of the contract, you'll pay a fee or charge. And that brings us to something called a 1035 Exchange. Section 1035 of the IRS Code allows you to exchange an existing annuity for a new annuity without paying any taxes on the income or capital gains.

Why would anyone choose to do that? Quite simply the new contract might be more advantageous. But be careful. You may incur surrender charges doing a 1035 exchange if the surrender period has not expired. And here's another consideration; the new annuity may have higher surrender charges and annual fees than the old annuity you just exited. Yes, insurance companies want to hold on to your money; yes, there is no such thing as a free lunch; and yes, it pays to look, listen and ask questions before you enter into any long-term contract, not just annuities. And that's exactly what most annuities are, long-term contracts.

Insurance companies and banks and mutual funds all want to hold onto your money. Nor should it surprise you that these groups have some of the most powerful lobbying organizations in Washington. And Washington, in case you have not noticed, is purely about politics. To suggest that this is a complete discussion of annuities would be almost as deceptive as a bunch of class action attorneys loitering around a banana peel convention. And speaking of lawyers, here is the definition of a tragedy: A bus load of attorneys going over a cliff with an empty seat. So to reiterate something we said earlier; annuities have their place in the investment world, but like Limburger cheese (whew!) they are not for everyone. It's your job to make sure they are for you.

CHAPTER TEN

The easiest person to deceive is oneself.

Edward Bulwer-Lytton

SLEEPING OR JUMPING

After the 1929 stock market crash, so painful and pervasive was the carnage, whenever anyone would check into a New York City hotel, the joke then making the rounds on radio (remember they didn't have television), went like this:

Guest: I'd like a room.

Clerk: For sleeping or jumping?

All good humor has a serious message buried inside. Good news, bad news jokes are rife, but there is much to be said for "telling it," as was the popular term in the 1960s, "like it is." One of the major characteristics of political correctness is to avoid "telling it like it is." It's almost as if kindness or deception has become a surrogate for the truth. How else can one explain such terms as homeless for street people? The late Los Angeles mayor Thomas Bradley, hardly a conservative, while still in office conducted his own survey of the so-called homeless in Los Angeles. Quite to his surprise, and those of his political lackeys, though they won't want to admit it, he discovered that one third of those on the street were there owing to circumstances beyond their control; another third were there owing to mental illnesses; and a full one-third were there, hard as it was and is for some to accept, because they wanted to and chose to be there. Isn't that the essence of America: freedom of speech and choice?

The problem with politicians is that they are, for the most part, not content with deceiving themselves. In the May 10, 2004 issue of *Forbes*, James Grant, a noted bear and advocate of owning some gold other than that used as dental fillings, wrote an essay called "The Fed's Folly" about central bankers and their apparent susceptibility for self-deception. The editor of *Grant's Interest Rate Observer*, Grant's thesis was simple and to the point: Most of these government employees, after all that is what they really are, talk as if they own an economic crystal ball. They speak as if they know what will happen beforehand and how we the folks at large should react and how what they see is in our benevolent interests, if only we trust their prophesizing. Think here about WMDs and slam-dunks.

The real coin of the realm, according to these bureaucrats, is in government employees we should trust. Grant goes on to raise an important issue: Why do we as a society tolerate these federal employees setting something as critical to our daily lives as short-term interest rates? After all, we don't allow a bunch of government workers to set the price of stocks, soybeans, sow bellies, wheat, oil or automobiles. And unless you live in the Peoples' Republic of Santa Monica, we don't allow governments to set the price of rents or houses. "There is," as Grant notes, "a vast futures market devoted to the price of credit. Why should a government committee set short-term interest rates?" The title of central bankers is just, as Grant says, a more highbrow term for federal worker, but the bottom line is they are still government hacks. And in this case government hacks who can wreak severe damage, especially when they prove less than omniscient, a proposition Grant believes (and we concur) that has much better than even odds of becoming fact.

These are not only people with big credentials but large egos, a prime recipe for self-deception if there ever was one. Several years ago we came across a sign in a chest surgeon's office that read: "Nothing is more dangerous than the state of absolute certainty." If you're thinking George Dubya here, you need to toss in Al Gore, the Kyoto Treaty and all of those the-earth-is-melting worry wonders. Both sides appear absolutely sure they are among the anointed. When it comes to one of the world's most famous stock pickers, however, self-deception doesn't seem to play much of a role. As a matter of fact, one could argue that self-deception and anti-competition are complete opposites.

Warren Buffett, the Moat Man, openly admits to seeking companies where competition is difficult. Such quasi-anti-trust policies don't appear to disturb Moat Man's sense of fair competition or fair play. After all, here's a guy who thinks property owners in California should pay higher taxes because the taxes on his land-locked Omaha digs are higher than those on his sea-side chalet north of San Diego. Buffet's philosophy suggests that he subscribes to what's been labeled as the capital cycle approach to investing. What we mean by capital cycle is when companies become hot, as they did during the tech bubble, valuations tend to soar. Rich valuation levels in the form of exorbitant stock prices deceive managements into investing more into the company. Investing more money eventually leads to glut. Glut is to falling prices as scarcity is to rising demand. But there is an even more subtle lesson here: it's not the bad ideas that do you in, a bad idea will become apparent soon enough; it's the good ideas gone bonkers. Read the *Great Gatsby*. It's really about a dream, probably not a bad idea initially, too fervently held onto too long.

It becomes part of the just build-it-and-they-will show up school. Price it and they will pay it. Perhaps the prime example of this during the bubble years was fiber optic cable; they laid enough of that stuff to fill up the Grand Canyon. In fact, one of the major themes of that era was companies knew best what to do with all the money they were raking in. That dividends were out and capital investment was in became the mantra of the time. It came as close to a state of absolute certainty as any in history. In a word, small fast growing companies attract competition that eventually drives returns or profits back to the mean.

Mature companies as a rule reflect a decline in competition. Perhaps this explains Buffett's forays into firms like Dexter, a shoe manufacturer; Acme Brick pavers; Benjamin Moore, a paint producer, carpet maker Shaw, World Book encyclopedias; and house wares company Pampered Chef not to mention furniture, mattresses and manufactured housing, while overtly rejecting throughout the 1990s fast-growing tech firms like Microsoft. When asked, Buffett usually claims that he avoided tech stocks because he and his partner Charlie Munger don't understand them. Perhaps the truth is he understands those rapid growing tech jobbies all too well. Nor do you have to be heavily into advertising to recognize that Buffett-type stocks have about as much sex appeal as an electric golf cart.

Why do we even bring this up? The reason is simple: many investors pray for the next Microsoft or Wal-Mart, hoping to get in on the ground floor and ride the stock up 10,000 or 20,000 percent over the next generation. Buffett appears for the most part to shun these small, fast-growing wunderkinds for well-established firms that show little sign of future growth. And that poses a question you as an investor should consider. Is it better to invest in smaller, faster-growing companies where competition is on the rise or old, stodgier firms where competition is dropping? Numerous studies have shown that of all the small, exciting growth-potential firms that come to the fore, very few ever turn into Microsoft or Wal-Mart.

Now we realize some of this may seem a bit esoteric. But as an old professor of ours used to say: "You have to always know more than what you're teaching." And investing is in our minds not much different. So you must decide, to bring this full circle, if you are a sleeper or a jumper or perhaps a little bit of both.

CHAPTER ELEVEN

How can you trust people who are poor and own no property?....
Inequality of property will exists as long as liberty exists.

Alexander Hamilton

REAL ESTATE

It is an interesting footnote that Mr. Hamilton, along with John Adams, was one of the founding fathers of the Federalist Party, which favored the adoption of the Constitution and the establishment of a strong, centralized government; in short, a government given to meddling in the affairs of its citizens. So which would you prefer, given Mr. Hamilton's edict, property for all with liberty for none or liberty for all with the possibility for many to accumulate some property? In our opinion, Mr. Hamilton was talking about folks having the liberty to be stupid and to do stupid things, like not being frugal enough to someday purchase property, something the current politically-correct trend is trying its best to abolish.

If all politics is local, as the late speaker of the House, Massachusetts Democrat Tip O'Neil once noted, many of you have heard that the *sine qua non* of real estate investing is location, location, location. Seaside property should appreciate more, barring hurricanes and tsunamis, than property located in the middle of the desert, that is, unless you've been investing in Las Vegas property of late. Between 2003 and 2004, for example, the median price for a home in the gambling Mecca accelerated 52.8 percent, the highest in the nation. Real estate comes in different packages, raw land, residential, commercial. Rental property can be subdivided again, commercial, apartments, family dwellings, pick your poison. Real estate also, like some equities, offers the possibility of a double-barrel payoff, capital gains and income, again pick your hemlock.

Given the politically correct drift of Congress over the past generation, however, there is little evidence that these elected officials favor the little guy real estate entrepreneur despite their fervent claims about how fervently they care about the little folks. So be aware real estate investing has it own unique pitfalls, not the least of which is politicians and the Internal Revenue Service. Still there is another way to play the real estate game; it's called Real Estate Investment Trusts or REITs. REITs are traded on stock exchanges. And they can run the gamut from industrial to shopping centers to residential properties to lease-backs to you name it. By law REITs are required to payout 90 percent of their income or cash flow and so they usually offer investors higher-than-normal dividends compared to other equities. Between 1999 and 2004 REITs outperformed the S&P 500 and they paid handsome dividends along the way. Is that where you want to invest now, maybe not? REITs have had a pretty good run, interest rates are headed higher and real estate fundamentals currently look on the weak side, depending who is doing the looking. In other words REITs, like people and business and the weather, go through cycles too. Your job as an investor, should you choose to accept it, is to figure out where we are in the cycle

One of the things you need to grasp about real estate investing is this: In the U.S. real estate has a decided regional ring to it. If in 1980 you put $100,000 into Massachusetts real estate by 2000 you would have seen the value increase to $660,000, the highest appreciation of any state for the period, including California. Not a bad return for having to suffer through the bloviatings of rosaceous-faced old Teddy. But the numbers can be misleading. Had you waited til 1989 to put that 100K to work in the Constitution State, you wouldn't have seen a profit until 1997. Even in the white-hot California market during the 1990s not all regions got treated the same. After the Internet bubble of Silicon

Valley burst real estate values in San Jose actually declined. Proximity counts. Isn't that what infectious disease and second hand smoke are all about?

Years ago we met an old commodity trader we'll call Harry. During his career Harry traded everything from wheat to wives. And Harry's track record was as good if not better than gold. A shy, introverted guy, it was not in Harry's genetic code to boast. Plucking information out of Harry was like pulling out champagne corks. And Harry kept records, meticulous, green eye shade-type records. He knew the price of cotton in1934 and the date, September 24, 1955, a Saturday, Ike had his famous heart attack and the market tanked on opening the following Monday.

One day over a cup of coffee in the early 1980s when we were complaining about high gasoline prices at the pump, Harry just smiled and reminded us that the cure for high prices is high prices, something government flacks never seem to get. We bring this up to highlight two points, one about oil and the other about real estate. Though they could tick higher, in early September/ October 2004 oil hit $52-plus a barrel, it could be for this cycle the peak. (By early fall of 2005 oil price hit $70 a barrel!) Anything is possible; Bill Clinton could come out tomorrow promoting celibacy, too. But we rather doubt it. The second point is high prices don't occur in a vacuum; high prices cause people to eventually alter their behavior.

In mid-2004 the *New York Times* ran an article about the increase in homeowners who are opting to sell their own home rather than pay the high commissions charged by real estate agents. In 2002 some 14 percent, or one in seven, sold their own homes, up from 13 percent in 2001. Though the peak was 19 percent in 1999, according to the National Association of Realtors, it is a growing trend. Lately there has been an explosion of Websites devoted to informing sellers how to do it, prompting the association to predict the numbers could soon reach one in four. With home prices soaring around the nation, it makes perfect sense. Paying six percent commission, pretty much the industry standard, on a $400,000 home can, like a surgeon's scalpel, cut pretty deep. Other commission-based industries have also felt the sting that higher prices bring. Think travel agents and commission-based insurance agents, to name a couple.

Economists expend a lot of verbiage talking about two concepts, elasticity and inelasticity. Now don't get yourself twisted into a big soft pretzel here. It's just terminology. Have the higher gas prices at the pump caused many folks to cut back on their driving, probably not. And the reason is simple. People need energy to get around everyday, go to work, the store, take the kids to soccer, to visit their physicians. So the price of gasoline is pretty much inelastic, meaning most of us will pay whatever the market bears. Prescription drugs for the most part fall into the inelastic category, too. (Yea, we know Congress is considering interfering. But the paradox here is by allowing in Canadian drugs their talking about opening up competition, a free market principle.) If prices jump too high on non-essential items, however, think haircuts and hotdogs, people will cut back on buying these products or services. It's what economists call elasticity. Jack up the price too high and consumers will exercise their Houdini option and disappear. And you can bet that's been one of Greenspan's biggest concerns since the stock market crash and 911 that consumers would pull a Houdini. So interest rates, whether you get it or not, are subject to the laws of elasticity. Crank rates high enough and folks (companies) will quit borrowing and consuming.

Now some pundits will argue that housing prices are inelastic. People want to own their chunk of the American dream irrespective. Well, maybe they do and maybe they don't; with rising home prices and the threat of rising inflation and higher interest rates, we're going to find out. What you need to do, to put it in totally capitalistic American terms, is figure out which scenario proves correct, so you can book a little profit on it. Yes, we said profit, a term the politically correct Michael Moores of the world love to hate in public but privately caress with both arms.

You might also want to historically compare real estate with other types of investments. So let's take a little side trip down history lane and compare real estate to stock and bonds and gold. Yes, we said gold. Why gold? Because it garners much attention, particularly in times of rising inflation, and everyone should own a little gold. Gold is a precious metal versus non-precious metals like lead and aluminum and platinum. But the word precious is relative here. See how precious, say, aluminum or platinum become if there is a shortage. Gold is considered a commodity like aluminum and platinum and lead and corn and wheat and soybeans. Gold is basically used in dentistry and industry. Of course, there is gold jewelry from gold-plated to the18 karat-stuff; and gold coins have been around since the Roman Empire.

Why do we bring this up? Because you hear—or probably have heard much talk about asset allocation, particularly among financial planners, a relatively new profession that came of age with the last big bull stock market. But since gold topped out in 1980 around $850 an ounce, most of the asset allocation has centered on paper assets as in stocks and bonds. In fact, the bull market in stocks that ended in 2000 actually began in 1982. Consider these numbers 777, 2592, 11,700? That's where DJIA sat in August 1982, at the end of 1995 and at the top of February 2000. So what's the point? Simply this: A whole generation of financial planners have sprouted since 1980 whose only idea of asset allocation until quite recently has been financial assets; and gold usually does well when these financial assets under perform.

As the chart below shows many commodities by the beginning of 2004 were up considerably from their bear market lows. And many have continued to appreciate since then, but it was the rare financial planner who back in early 2004 was touting commodities to his or her clients.

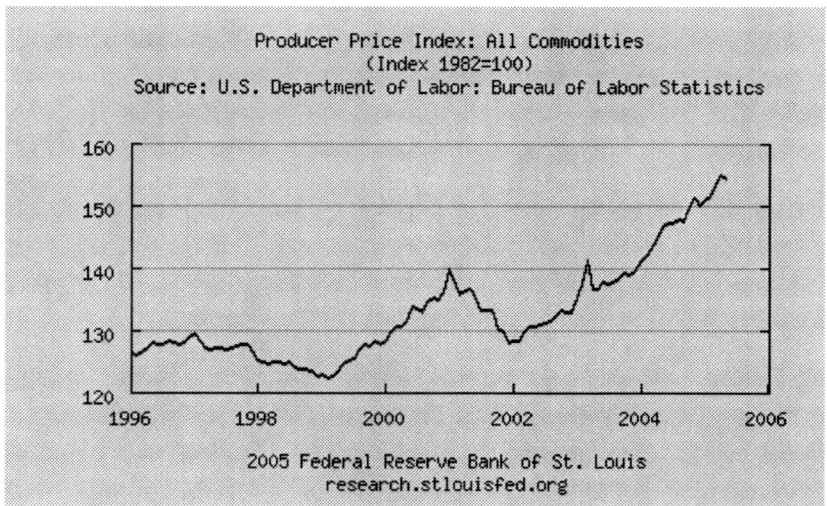

Producer Price Index: All Commodities
(Index 1982=100)
Source: U.S. Department of Labor: Bureau of Labor Statistics

2005 Federal Reserve Bank of St. Louis
research.stlouisfed.org

But you thought we were discussing real estate and we are. Since its zenith in 1980 at $850 an ounce the yellow stuff has traded all over the place but mostly lower as in a lot lower. Before its recent run-up to $500 an ounce, gold changed hands a couple of years earlier around $278. "For the past 30 years," writes Jim Rogers in his 2004 book *Hot Commodities*, "gold hasn't done all that great compared with other assets." Rogers then compares gold with real estate and the S&P 500 index. "If you bought a house in a decent spot in the New York City, Boston, or Los Angeles areas in the 1970s it might now be worth more than 20 times your original investment. Over the same period, the S&P 500 is up more than 3000% (reinvested dividends included)."

So for the last 30 years just about everything has glittered more than gold. Yes, you should own some. How much? The short answer is very little, about 5-10% of your portfolio. Gold belongs in your just-in-case asset allocation basket. Gold has two basic costs the price you pay to buy it and the price of holding or carrying it. And you probably thought only those darn kids who return to live at home after graduating from college had carrying costs. Here in California people buy earthquake insurance— just in case. Like gold it can be expensive. Now we realize that one is not suppose to toot one's own bassoon. But we would not be anything if we were not iconoclastic. In a February/March 2204 newsletter to our private clients we penned the following "There is a big misconception about gold, especially among the gold bugs. They say gold represents a store of value. Not so. Gold is a hedge, like an insurance policy. And like an insurance policy gold only represents a hedge for the period that it is held. And right now is a good time to be holding some. An insurance policy can only increase in value if something unfortunate happens to the person or the item the policy is insuring. In short, it's a "put option." And by holding some gold, some oil and some other commodities right now the item your insuring is your purchasing power, the U.S. dollar."

Though for the average investor playing commodities has been rather difficult, it is getting easier. Now some mutual fund companies such as Pimco and Oppenheimer offer retail investors a way to get some exposure, and there will certainly be more in the future.

And before you run out to vote during the next election, local or otherwise, to vote for some politician who wants to invoke price controls or more government regulation, consider this. There are no guarantees, especially when it comes to politicians. Today real estate enjoys some tax advantages; that might not always be the case. So do your homework and be on the lookout for Trojan horses full of regulations designed to make it all better.

CHAPTER TWELVE

The political machine triumphs because it is a united minority acting against a divided majority.

Will Durant

POLITICS

If the above quote doesn't sum up our current two party apparatus then you need to clean the cerumen from your ears and drop some Visine in your eyes.

As mentioned in the chapter on risks, investment risks come in many ways, interest rates, credit, market and so on. One of the biggest risks is political. Though it is sometimes called geopolitical, politics is still at the core. Many Americans have difficulty comprehending that here in this country we have political risks. What usually comes to mind when we think about geopolitical risks is some dictator in some third world banana republic seizing or nationalizing property owned by foreign companies. The truth is that investors here in the U.S. are no less subject to political risk (or what some have called political blackmail) than any other nation despite cries to the contrary. If you think otherwise then you have not been paying attention to some of the eminent domain cases going on around the nation where Americans are having their property confiscated by local municipalities to build town homes or shopping malls. And that brings us to what we call the three Ps of investing—**politics, position and premium**.

But that's getting a bit ahead of the story. If you don't think that political risk in America exists and, moreover, can hurt your chances for investing success, you have not been paying attention to the tobacco and asbestos cases, just to name a couple of incidents. Irrespective of what your views about tobacco and smoking are, the politics got ugly and serious. With asbestos, perfectly viable companies were forced into bankruptcy, killing hundreds and in some cases, thousands of jobs. Which conjures up an interesting point: to some, outsourcing jobs is evil, killing them via litigation seems to trouble very few.

Many of these companies were guilty of nothing more than purchasing another firm that in some instances had been in the asbestos business more than 25 years earlier but were no longer manufacturing or selling asbestos. But that didn't stop those greedy trial lawyers. In other words, you could be held responsible for a malpractice incident that you didn't even commit nearly a quarter of a century earlier simply by association. In the tobacco settlements, more than half the money never went to the so-called intended purposes that were cited to justify the legal action in the first place. If you and I did this, we'd been brought up for fraud. And many people would point to the Alternative Minimum Tax as a form of political risk. Called AMT, the tax was invoked to ensure that the so-called wealthy pay their fair share (there's that word again) of taxes. Trouble is, like most legislation, the law ensnared the unsuspecting and the innocent. And to compound it all, politicians have no intentions of righting the wrong anytime soon because the government now needs the money, what with national security costs skyrocketing and the budget deficit rearing its so-called ugly puss again.

Fail to learn this at your own peril: fairness is the bête noir of simplicity. Perfect fairness is akin to zero risk. They only exist in the pathetic, misguided minds of know-it-all bureaucrats and politicos and social engineers. As a good friend years ago disturbingly put it: "Life is a terminal illness."

There have been numerous studies since the seat belt law went into effect showing that, though the seriousness of injuries in car collisions is down, the number of accidents has significantly increased. The reason: because drivers feel safer they drive faster and with more reckless abandon. In other words, they drive beyond their actual driving skills. If you really wanted to make drivers slow down, drive safer and consume less fuel (no small matter given the run-up in oil prices in 2003 and 2004 and 2005) every new car would be manufactured with an assegai attached to the steering wheel with a huge, scalpel-sharp arrow head pointed directly at the driver's left ventricle. It would also put the squeeze on rear-end collisions. But then you'd probably have all those body shop workers picketing in the nation's unemployment lines, protesting the outsourcing of jobs. And if you think driving, like most other activities in life, doesn't involve a certain amount of skill, you have never watched a NASCAR race. It is a false belief based on a false premise, something you'll find yourself facing in investing many times if you are paying attention.

And here again if you need an example, just think about the Internet; it was going to make everyone rich and everyone could do it. Sir John Templeton, perhaps one of the greatest investors of all time, has said that the five most dangerous words in the investing world are: "It's different this time!" People who over-estimate their driving skills owing to seat belts are no different from the Internet bubble crowd. Both bought into the belief that such things change the fundamental precepts of risk management.

So make no mistake, politics matter. When it comes to investing, the two Ps, as already noted, are **politics** and **position**. First figure out the politics and then put on your position. If you get the politics correct, more often than not your position will do just fine. In the summer of 2003 much of the eastern United States experienced a serious blackout. Since the blackout affected New York or The Big Apple, the screaming, as expected, became particularly strident. Politicians were falling out of their pulpits to find a villain. And as usual few suggested that our astute elected officials do what most of the rest of us have to do most of the time when we're seeking the culprit--gaze into a mirror. One of the utility companies involved in the blackout was First Energy in Ohio. The stock promptly dropped almost as fast as Massachusetts Senator John Kerry changes his mind. Some astute investors went sniffing around and determined the cry was worse than the hue and made some serious money.

Politics and their effect on investments are not always so obvious. In early 2002 Stanley Works, a Connecticut tool company founded more than 150 years ago, won overwhelming shareholder approval to move its head office to Bermuda. The company's reasons: to cut costs and increase profits. Implied in the board of directors' announcement was a not-so cryptic message about high taxes and over regulation. Within hours of the firm's declaration, many leftists and not a few on the right in Congress rolled out the name calling bandwagon: "Traitors!" "Profiteers!" New York Congressman Charles Rangel, a noted left-winger, accused Stanley of choosing "profits over patriotism." Iowa Senator Charles Grassley, a Republican, claimed: "There is no business reason for doing this other than to escape U.S. taxation." Keep in mind that taxation is just another form of inflation.

Investment guru Warren Buffett is known by many monikers, the Sage of Omaha, the Omaha Scold, to name a couple. Around the same time Stanley was getting a media and political tongue-lashing, the Omaha Oracle was loading up on the euro, on its way to a low of 82-cents, buying when the currency hit 86-cent to the U.S. dollar. And he kept buying until the euro reached $1.20. In December 2004 the fledgling currency topped the $1.35 mark against good old Uncle Sam's perceived not-so-good-anymore greenback. Between January 2002 and the start of 2005, the dollar declined 33 percent against the euro. Buffett blamed the dollar's downfall "on bad policy coming from both the White House and Congress." In Buffett's own words it was a $20 million vote of no confidence against U.S. fiscal policy. Now if that sounds strangely reminiscent of what Stanley Works was saying, you're on to something. And by his own admission Buffett continued to buy, something many might see as un-American. But Buffett, a known leftist supporter, makes a fortune of nearly $400 million for his firm and their shareholders shorting the U.S. dollar and that is different. By helping to push the dollar lower to book a profit for his firm and his shareholders, Buffett was also pushing up the price of imports; in other words, creating inflation for Mr. Mrs. and Ms. Everyday America. Think the price of oil here; oil is, among several other commodities, denominated in dollars.

Certainly Buffett and his defenders will argue that he is just protecting his firm's huge holdings, $40 billion, of U.S. Treasury securities. Poor fiscal policy will make the value of those bonds worth less, so Buffett is in fact hedging and in the long run is really bullish on America, according to him. Warren Buffett's investment company, Berkshire Hathaway, has two classes of shares, A and B. The A shares closed 2004 trading around $89,000 a share. That's right; you're reading it correctly, $89,000 a single share! The B shares closed around $3,000 a share. Now rewind quickly to Stanley Works. Stanley wanted to move its home office to Bermuda to cut costs, increase the bottom line and increase their shareholders' value. Increasing shareholder value is another way of saying protecting their investments.

Now what makes this interesting is Buffett openly affiliates with politicians on the left, politicians who claim they really care about the little gals and guys of America. Many of these little people are the same folks who regularly shop at Wal-Mart, the huge discount chain that makes it profits promoting cheap goods imported from China and the rest of Asia. By shorting the dollar Buffett helped push up the prices of those cheap goods. But there is still another point here. When Stanley announced its decision to move it estimated it would save $30 million a year. We don't know about you, but that sounds like a pretty compelling business reason to us. Think about earnings driving stock prices here. And about those shareholders, just who were they? Well at the time, according to Yahoo! Finance, five of the largest shareholders were mutual funds like Vanguard Index 500 Fund and Fidelity and T. Rowe Price. Now here's a little quiz for you? How many people, everyday people like you and me and your neighbor, do think at the time owned shares in mutual funds, particularly the largest, most poplar index fund in America, versus those who could afford to own Buffet's class A or B shares?

Warren Buffett is an investment icon. Nearly 20,000 worshippers show up at his annual meeting in Omaha to hear him and his partner Charley Munger pontificate. It's a fairly safe bet that few are regular Wal-Mart shoppers. It is also a safe bet that, in taking on Buffett, we can't be accused of starting a tussle with a puny paperweight. To say that Buffett by shorting the dollar didn't realize he was sticking it to the little guys and girls, those folks his political cronies claim they care so much about, is to deny reality. It's akin to saying Sir Alan Greenspan didn't know he was ripping all those COLA folks and seniors living on fixed incomes when he dropped interest rates to historical lows and kept them there to fight phantom deflation. Buffett's $20 million dollar bet against the dollar alone was hardly enough to drop the dollar in a currency market that trades $1 trillion dollars a day. But it's like the proverbial straw; everyone always talks about it, but few can actually identify the one that does the actual damage.

Now not everyone will agree with this assessment, but that shouldn't surprise you. When it comes to investing if you are going to wait for everyone to agree on your position, you are going to miss most of the good opportunities. One of American poet Robert Frost's most famous poems, "The Road not Taken," ends with: "Somewhere ages and ages hence; two roads diverged in a wood and I: -I took the one less traveled by; And that has made all the difference." The world loves to promote conformity. View the European Union's constant carping about George W. Bush's so-called unilateralism or the global environmental thugs pointing the finger of guilt at the United States for failing to sign the Kyoto treaty, a document nearly as flawed as Al Gore's personality.

Though many give it lip service, few people actually have either the inclination or the courage to pursue Frost's dictum. Yet much of the world's advancements, whether it's science, medicine, or human affairs, owe their origins to people who dared to take that less-traveled path.

Society promotes the idea of conformity, as well it should to a certain point. In the world of investing, however, conformity for the most part is just another name for mediocrity; the only difference is one begins with an m, the other with a c.

We previously mentioned investors seeking the next small stock wonder hoping it will magically morph into the next hot Wall Street goliath. Take a look at biotech companies. Anyone with an idea and some venture capital can start a biotech firm, and that's exactly what you're buying, an idea. Thousands gets started, but how many survive to make real money for real investors. Most of them have as much chance of hitting a homerun as you do anytime soon of seeing Martha Stewart and Donald Trump starring in a sitcom on humility.

That no one has yet cornered the market on foolishness shouldn't surprise you: Witness western-style governments still trying to export Wilsonian-type democracy around the world. According to the history we read, since the dawn of man there has been something like 43,000 wars around the globe. Don't know about you, but that sounds like a secular trend to us. Folks have made tons of money going long wars. If all this sounds a bit harsh, or to use the terms preferred by the PC crowd, mean-spirited and strident, we suggest you reacquaint yourself with the word reality. Markets can be incorrect, but they hardly stay that way for long.

And if you think politics don't matter, gander at this chart about Social Security.

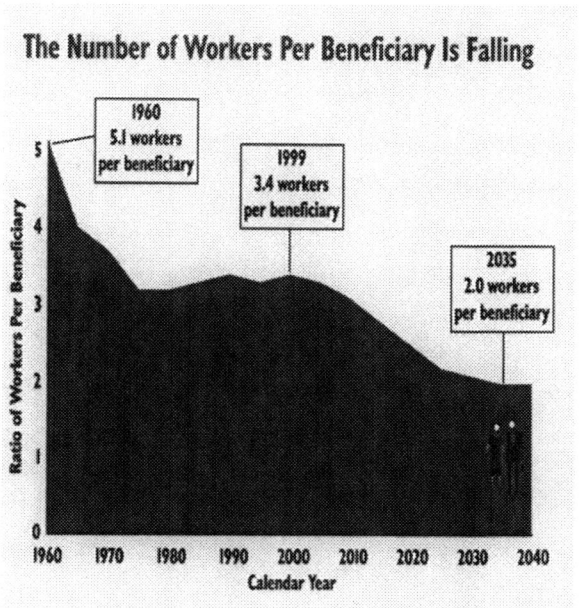

The Number of Workers Per Beneficiary Is Falling

Briefly, what it depicts is the number of younger workers compared to the number of retirees who will soon be drawing their Social Security as boomers start to enter their retirement years. Many experts feel that as the ratio of workers to dependents declines over the next several years, inflation will rise and the return on investment will decline. The current ratio is roughly 0.21 retirees to every worker; that number is set to almost double to 0.37 in the next 30 years. That will put big pressure on boosting the legal retirement age for Social Security assuming it survives. So if you're under 35 counting on Social Security to help you with your retirement may prove a pure form of folly, all the more reason to take command of your investing future. As Aldous Huxley noted: "There is only one corner of the universe you can be certain of improving, and that is your own self."

CHAPTER THIRTEEN

What I need is someone to make me do what I can

Ralph Waldo Emerson

ABILITY AND SELLING

Hara Haci Bu is an ancient Asian weight loss secret. It could just as easily, however, become an excellent principle for selling your winners in the stock market, assuming you ever again have any, given the carnage many suffered between 2000 and 2003. Big losses carry big psychological scars. Hara Haci Bu followers, mostly elders, live on an island off the coast of Japan. The premise is simple: stop eating when you are 80 percent full.

According to Hara Haci Bu acolytes, it takes the stomach roughly 20 minutes to signal the brain that the point of satiation has been reached. At the first sign of getting that full feeling, Hara Haci Bu practitioners stop shoveling in the fuel and wait 20 minutes. Waiting 20 minutes helps the body feel satisfied and aids in cutting down on unwanted calories. It also helps these people consume between 10 percent and 40 percent fewer calories than their American counterparts. Overindulgence at the feeding trough can, as nearly everyone realizes, shorten life. And except for a few poets, martyrs and artists, who wants a short life? Studies show people frequently eat their way into a variety of health problems ranging from diabetes to cardiovascular disease. In June 2002 *The Wall Street Journal* noted that scientists today are unraveling the secrets of longevity. It appears that the key to living a longer life is following a diet scientists have labeled "calorie restriction."

Calorie restriction ostensibly causes biochemical changes in the body that have a greater effect on life span than just avoiding diseases caused by consuming too much fat. Scientists first stumbled on this while doing rat research in the 1930s. Well-fed rats kept lean by regular exercises, researchers discovered, don't necessarily increase their maximum life span, but they do avoid dying prematurely from the diseases that well-fed, sedentary rats experience. Even more striking, caloric intake matters most. Rats fed a calorie restriction diet actually lived longer. City rats grow twice as fast as their non-city brethren and weigh 40 percent more, reaching a maximum of 20 inches and two pounds. Perhaps it is owing to all the garbage or "junk food" available in the big cities. More important, scientists were later able to demonstrate the same results in guppies, spiders, water fleas and yeast. In early 2002 the largest mammal ever, Labrador retrievers, joined the growing list. And now researchers are close to showing that monkeys fed a caloric restriction diet also exhibit extended life spans.

What makes this work so exciting is monkeys share about 90 percent of their genes with humans. According to the National Institute of Health, where researchers have been studying more than 100 rhesus monkeys for 15 years, evidence continues to support the idea that caloric restriction extends life span. Studies using humans are now underway. Though still early, results look promising. And that brings us back to the island off the coast of Japan, Okinawa. The diet most people eat there consists of rice, vegetables, soy and small amounts of fish and meat. Okinawa has 34 centenarians per 100,000 people, more than three times the number in the U.S. In fact, according to gerontologists, the oldest person in the world lives on an island nearby. He is 114.

During the last bull market, especially in recent years when investors painfully peruse the damage inflicted on their 401(k) plans when the big stock market dike ruptured, Hara Haci Bu is something many investors wish they had known about. Capturing 80 percent of a stock's run-up sure beats the gluttony of hanging around for that last morsel of extra profit. Remember the old, now trite rule, any positive integer multiplied times zero equals zero. And it doesn't matter which way—from right to left or left to right—you do the math. So the lesson should be clear: Eighty percent of something trumps 80 percent of nothing every time.

But learning to take your profits implies the need to time the market, something the gurus have been for years telling anyone who will listen no one can consistently do. The key word here is consistently. One of the major traps of the last bull market (indeed every bull market) is it kept going up long after many believed it would, going higher than most believed it could. That kind of upward thrust creates its own peril, not the least of which is it makes investors afraid to sell because they believe they will miss greater gains. And for a while it did make many who exited early miss those gains. It also leads to the mantra many mutual funds and brokerage firms love: Buy and hold or invest for the long term. Keep those assets under management so they can continue to earn those fees. If you have not guessed by now that much of Wall Street is about fees—fees to market IPOs, fees to cut investment banking deals, fees to buy and sell and so forth, you've been snoozing and that's probably in part why you have been losing. Put differently, bull markets inculcate against discipline. Investors become more concerned about losing the gains they have yet to receive than protecting the gains they already received. It's the inverse of the old saying: a bird in the hand is worth two in the bush. Not during bull markets.

To make money in the stock market you only need to be right 51 percent of the time. If you're correct 65 or 70 percent of the time, you'll need to back up a truck to haul away your winnings. Every investor's dream is to buy low and not sell high but sell at the peak. Yet almost nobody, professional, amateur or alien from the outer galaxies, ever sells a stock at its peak anymore than hordes of investors successfully exit the stock market at its peak. In reality, just the reverse is usually true. Yes, stocks undergo peaks and valleys during their historical undulations. Stocks are like people. If they've been around awhile, they have a history. Years ago right after I bought my first stock (It was all new to me!) I was somewhat surprised a few weeks later when I ran into a fellow who told me he had once owned that particular equity 15 years earlier.

Xerox is a well-known company. Here's a brief sketch of its history. The famous maker of copiers got into a bind in the late 1990s, trading at one point as low as $7 a share. It's currently changing hands around $14.85. Way back in 1966 when the stock market headed south so did Xerox's stock, trading on a split adjusted basis near $42 a share. By 1970, however, despite a severe bear market, the shares were selling at $116.

In those days, much like the highflying NASDAQ stocks of the 1990s, Xerox was perceived as a growth vehicle. But with the arrival of spring that year, Xerox followed the general market down, falling from $116 to $65 before the damage subsided. Just two short years later the market had rebounded and so had Xerox, rising more than 100 points to trade near $172. Xerox's upward explosion preceded the DJIA top of 1051.70 in the first quarter of 1973 by just a few months. Over the next 22 months the DJIA would surrender nearly 50% of its value, closing out 1974 at 616.24. With the 1973-74 bear market, Xerox joined its brethren Nifty Fifty members, taking the proverbial bath, falling below $50 a share.

After a brief rally coming out of the bear market, Xerox churned in a trading range for years. By 1981 when Xerox's earnings were estimated at $7 a share, a figure nearly six times greater than its earnings for 1966, the stock dropped below its 1966 price of $42. A year later earnings fell off and so did the stock price, declining to just $27. And as already noted by the late 1990s the stock was trading below $9 a share. Xerox to be sure was viewed early on in its existence as a high tech growth company. So given all the ranting and raving about technology and the new-age during the 1990s, Xerox's history brings to mind something Harry Truman once said: "The only thing new today is the history you failed to learn yesterday."

The Xerox story illustrates a basic market principal that many investors fail to understand, the statistical law of regression to the mean. If you were to take a 15 or 20-year fix on Xerox's average price, chances are better than good that it would fall somewhere between the all-time low and the all-time high. So the obvious conclusion is that Xerox's stock experienced times when it was expensive and times when it was cheap compared to its historical average price. Like it or not, deciding when something, a stock or otherwise, is cheap or expensive becomes a timing decision. How do you tell when prices are low or stocks are cheap? Well, we just told you. Where is the item, in this case the stock, selling in relation to its historical average price? Choose any period you want, 5-year, 10-year, 15-year, most likely the longer the better. Though hardly a new indicator is the dividend yield on the S&P 500 index. Some market followers use the dividend yield on the S&P 500 index to gage whether stocks are cheap or dear, though it is hardly foolproof. Still it pays to do your homework. You might want to get familiar with its historical averages. However, as the Xerox story demonstrates prices can go down or up or remain flat often times longer than one thinks.

Here is a ten-year look back at the NASDAQ 100.

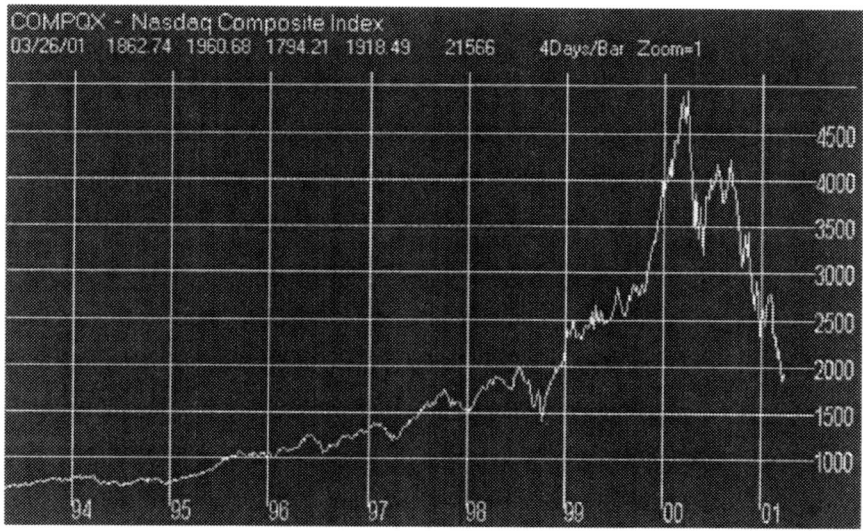

Blasingham and Ellison Financial Group

An interviewer once asked comedian Billy Crystal about his years on *Saturday Night Live* and the characters he portrayed. Much of the show was pure improvisation. "I loved the danger of it," Crystal responded, "that it was on the air." And that's a trait all good traders and good stock investors share; they love the danger of it, that it is live, not a dress rehearsal. Make no mistake loving the danger of it is completely antipodal to being addicted to the action. All addictions debilitate. Loving the danger of it and putting in place contingency strategies to limit your risk is characteristic of true professionals. True amateurs, on the other hand, fail to grasp the need for contingency plans like placing trailing stop loss orders. Remember this: the name of the game is about profits, not excitement.

There are all kinds of orders when buying stocks—good until cancel orders, limit buy and sell orders, market orders, all or none, partial orders. A trailing stop loss order (TSL) simply means you try to put a floor under your potential losses or gains. Say you purchase 100 shares of a stock for $20 and you concomitantly place a trailing stop loss order to sell the stock at a price six percent below $20 or at a price of $18.80, essentially limiting your downside risk to a buck twenty or six percent of the your purchase price of $20. Now if bad came to worst and you had three consecutive trades were you lost five or six percent on each you would be down 15 percent or so. For purposes of clarity let's just say on your next trade you got stopped out again using your six percent stop loss order, but this time with a 25 percent gain. In total you made four trades with only one profitable, but you are (minus trading costs; they always have to be calculated) up seven percent. You had three losing trades, each costing you six percent and one winning trade where you gained 25 percent. The point here is you move your trailing stop loss order up as the stock price rises. This takes discipline and some understanding of the volatility of the particular stock you are interested in or buying.

Without those TSL orders on the losing trade you could've found yourself down by a much larger amount. Deciding to use TSL orders is up to you. Also up to you is deciding what percentage of loss you'll feel comfortable taking. It's a safe bet, however, that whatever that percentage is it won't match what many retail investors suffered after the Internet bubble burst.

Whipsawed is one of the warnings you will hear gurus spout whenever you suggest using TSL orders. As J.P. Morgan once noted when asked what the stock market would do in the future (His reply: "It will fluctuate!"), stock prices change or vary. If you bought a stock at 30 because you believed it was headed to 50 and you get stopped out at, say, 28 and it climbs to 32 before you can get back in and it does go to 50, how much have you lost? On the other hand, it you don't place a TSL order, the stock drifts to 25 before you get disgusted and sell out, then promptly rallies to 35 on it's way to 50, your original target and belief, how much are you out? Investors are chary about re-buying a stock above what they originally paid, never quite understanding that averaging into a position is one of the better ways to make money, assuming your initial premise proves correct. Now right here we need to say something about averaging down.

Many gurus will advise against averaging down; that is, buying a stock as its price continues to decline. The analogy they love to use is "trying to catch a falling knife." Like a lot of those pithy-sounding stratagems, it's similar to many of those half-truths we all learned in college. The correct answer is: it depends. The examples of people buying stocks when their prices were declining and then going on to make fortunes when prices reversed are legion. Problem is so are the examples of those who purchased stock on the way down only to see them stay down or, worse yet, go belly-up. About all one can say is this has to do with risk tolerance and, corny and trite as it sounds, doing your homework.

Paradoxical as it may sound, those who have the most discipline in life have the most freedom. It's a point few really understand. Say you usually workout at the gym in the mornings but for whatever reasons decide to put it off for later in the day. You subsequently get busy and begin to wonder if you'll have time later to get the workout in. As time passes the whole thing sort of hangs fire and next you start having those guilty twangs most of us get when we delay things that we could have done earlier. Convoluted as it may appear, the only way to have a lot of freedom is to have a lot of discipline. That's why much of the advice shoveled down the gullets of retail investors during the bull run of 1997-2000, anyone can do it and anyone can do it with only 30 minutes a week, smacked of cataleptic Wall Street cant.

Some of you may be old enough to remember those magazine ads years ago about Charles Atlas, the world's strongest man, who had a training course to keep bullies at the beach from kicking sand in weaklings' faces. To be successful even old Charley's program required 20 minutes of exercise a day 7 days a week. To be certain, there are some tough bullies out there, but even the toughest is hardly as tough to deal with as the stock market. Once again the 30-minute nonsense is part of the free pretzels and beer belief promoters love to promote.

So here is the key thing to remember: it's the questions you ask, not the answers you get; and in the stock market it's not the price you pay when you buy so much as it is the price you get when you sell. That's another way out pointing out that it's not the small losses that hurt you so much; it's the huge hits. You can't afford to take many of them either in life, the ring or the market. So remember your Hara Haci Bu. It will prevent you from becoming fat and poor. To put the Hara Haci Bu in stock market parlance; it is the gastronomic version of an old story about Baron Rothchild, the famous billionaire. When asked how he made his money in the market, Rothchild replied: "By selling too soon."

CHAPTER FOURTEEN

Knowledge is free at the library; just bring your own container

Anonymous

KNOWLEDGE

The same today could just as easily be said about the Internet. What you really need to know is: 2Cs + 2Ls + 3Ps + 3Vs plus one little ole lonely S. No, this isn't pre-calculus math or some esoteric formula for the latest ephedrine-free fat burner. But if you can grasp this material you'll be well on your way to treading more safely through the calculus-like shoals of the market. So what do the two Cs stand for? **Credit** and **Correlation,** and we realize that's what you were thinking all along. Remember in the first chapter we discussed credit and in the chapter on bonds the subject cropped up again. We mentioned risk. It turns out that risk is Janus-faced; it can be good and, as we noted way back in chapter one, it can create havoc, not to mention occasionally firing up those lachrymal glands. A borrower may default, something market pundits call default event risk (reread chapter on risks!). That's pretty simple. A borrower, for whatever reasons, decides to walk. The other face of credit you'll understand more clearly when we discuss that little ole lonely S, **spread**, and its significance. But for now here is the answer. Even on an un-defaulted loan the lender incurs spread risk.

What does that mean? Well, take all that celebrating folks have been doing refinancing their mortgages when Alan Greenspan and his merry band of central bankers kept interest rates artificially low under the guise that they were heading off deflation. Most of those loans or refinances are sold in the secondary market; and the buyer of last resort is usually one of the quasi-government agencies (Also known as GSEs, government sponsored enterprises.) You probably know them as Fannie Mae or Freddie Mac.

It may be sweet music to your coin bag when you pre-pay your loan early and get a lower rate, but the owner of that loan has another problem: he or she has to re-invest those funds, almost always at a lower rate, and that cuts into his or her return. If you're thinking re-investment risk here, give yourself a slap on the posterior. You celebrate getting a higher return on your money and that is what refinancing at a lower mortgage rate provides you. Do you think that the buyer of your mortgage is any different? He would like to get the highest, safest return on his funds too.

So, many of these folks don't just sit there, especially in a falling interest rate scenario, hoping you and others like you won't refinance. They hedge the possibility by purchasing or going long Treasury bills and bonds. Remember Boyle's Law; falling interest rates cause bonds prices to rally. Mortgage rates for all intents and purposes are determined by the interest rates available on Treasury bonds. Call it the Federal Reserve Bank connection. (There is a correlation; remember that term because we'll be coming back to it soon.) So they offset the loss of that income with the possibility of capital appreciation. And as they say, all is well that ends well.

But often times that is not the way it works in the world of spreads and investing and interest rates. Should interest rates unexpectedly and suddenly spike higher, you can look for them to close those long bond positions, heading for the exits like a bunch of Mad Hatters. Who wants to get caught, especially where leverage is concerned, holding what is essentially billions of dollars of an asset that is losing value faster than most of today's high school (college) seniors can spell the word arbitrage. And by the way, when interest rates are rising, they can hedge by shorting those government bonds should they so choose to make up for lost income or lost purchasing power because they are stuck with all those low-mortgage rates they previously purchased and you and I are not in any hurry to refinance.

So if you are starting to hear a gurgling or bubbling sound somewhere in your distant gray matter, it just might be an age-old concept, a basic truth despite what many would have you accept, there are not any free lunches, coming to the surface of your investment consciousness. Let's say that again, just to irk all those know-it-all social engineers and politicians: there are no free lunches. And in a truly egalitarian society, not that this is one, neither should there be.

Nearly everything in life has a spread. Bedspreads, spreads that go on slices of bread; in the jewelry business its called keystone. When you buy a stock there is a bid and an ask price. The ask price is what you have to pay; the bid price is what you can sell the stock for. Here's an example. The stock XCA is quoted at 23 ¼ by 23 ½. The quarter point difference between the ask price of 23 1/4 and 23 ½ bid is the spread. So the stock has to rally by at least ¼ of point before you are even; and that's aside from commission charges since they are not included in the bid and ask quote. Now it turns out, all things equal, large stocks like those traded on the NYSE versus smaller ones like those traded on the NASDAQ have smaller spreads. And the same thing applies to many mutual funds and the rate your lender lends you the money to purchase your home. People in business to make money don't go around lending money to folks at their cost; they mark it up a bit. Call it the price of doing business. NASDAQ stocks tend to be small capitalization firms; smaller stocks tend to be more volatile and, as such, they tend to have a wider bid and ask spread than larger capitalization stocks. Again, folks like to be compensated for the risk.

Wow! You say that's nice, but tell us something we don't already know. Well, try this: Spreads have histories, just like diseases and just like you and me. All right, here's one for you. What's the historical spread on the yield of junk bonds versus the yield on U.S. Treasury bonds of comparable maturities? Or for that matter the yield between U.S. Treasury bonds and bonds of emerging country markets? Do spreads ever widen or narrow? Do they ever exceed their historical norm? And if they do what message is that sending us? And if spreads do widen or narrow or, for that matter, sometimes remain flat for quite a while, can we make any money from it?

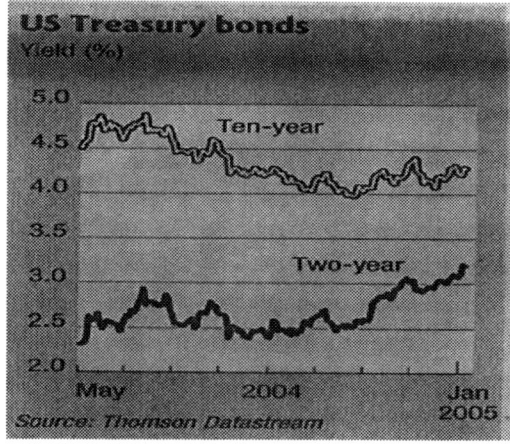

The chart above shows the narrowing spread between 10 year and 2 year Treasury Bonds between May 2004 and January 2005.

To end the suspense the answer is yes. Assuming you have an idea of what you're doing, you can make money from all three situations. If the yield spread between, say, junk bonds and U.S. Treasury bonds narrows dramatically below its historical average what's the implied message? Could it be signaling increased risk or giving off a sign that one should consider exiting those junk bonds for safer terrain? Could it be what many retirees found themselves facing since the stock market crash in 2000, and interest rates fell off a cliff, a bunch of yield-starved investors, forcing them to take on more risk to get the returns they need just to live? Are U.S. government bonds considered to be less risky than junk bonds? What is the implied message when, say, a patient's heart rate spikes either way below or way above the normal range?

As a health practitioner you are charged with knowing the normal; otherwise how are you going to be able to appreciate the abnormal? So that raises the question why is there a spread to begin with and the answer is simple. The spread is there because there is implied risk there. Go out and log a bunch of traffic tickets, minor infractions or no, and see what happens to the price of your auto insurance. It skyrockets because you are perceived as being more risky and folks want to be compensated for shouldering that risk. How is that any different from junk bonds or the debt of emerging market countries?

That second C stands for, if you have not already guessed it, **correlation**. Some things are correlated and others are not. Simple enough you say, but how about some examples? Well, here's one: the purchase of homes is correlated to interest rates; the lower interest rates fall, the more prospective homebuyers can qualify. That's called a positive correlation. Many stock markets are positively correlated to the U.S. stock market, meaning usually when the United States market rallies so do these particular markets. But some markets around the world don't rally when the U.S. market goes up. That's called negative correlation. A strong dollar is negatively correlated with the price of gold. (At least historically it has been!). Gold is considered to be an inflation hedge. So who needs to hedge inflation if the dollar is strong? A weak dollar translates into loss of purchasing power.

Another correlation related to purchasing power is time. If inflation averages only 3 percent per annum, after just 15 years you'll need 55 percent more income just to stay even on purchasing power. So you might want to pay attention to the historical average of inflation. In the early 1970s President Richard Nixon slapped on price controls with inflation at 3 percent. Exact measurements of the rate of inflation are difficult at best because of the built-in assumption of the consumer price index that something stable is being measured, not to mention most governments have more than a passing interest in keeping their subjects (the term citizen is a euphemism!) off balance when it comes to the real truth about inflation. The term hedonic should come to mind here, but that's another subject for you to look up. There is another apparent correlation between time and inflation. According to U.S. government statistics, consumer prices for people 62 years old and older have risen faster than the national average over that last 20 years. Now there is no guarantee that trend will continue. But then again there is no guarantee that it won't. For some readers 62 may be an age far down the pike, for others it may be that proverbial hop, skip and you-know-what away, but the implications for retirement planning should be clear.

Now we discussed inflation in a previous chapter and our purpose here is to inform not frighten. But holding inflation in check is important (Think governments fudging their numbers! That way the natives don't get too restive and they don't catch on quite as fast.) because from time to time hyperinflation has reared its ugly, devastating head. The Weidmar Republic in Germany during the 1920s is one example. In Yugoslavia in 1992 the national bank of Serbia issued single bank notes of 500 billion Serbian dinars. According to one account at the time, the citizens were in "a constant race against time to purchase whatever they could wherever there was anything to be bought. Prices increased at a rate of 2 percent per hour or 64 percent a day. In 1993 hyperinflation reached a record of 400,000 billion percent. In October of that year, 600 grams of pork cost 26 dinars, with the same amount costing 21 billion dinars three months later."

When the dollar weakens investors traditionally start looking toward gold. When real interest rates (Remember them: nominal rates minus inflation equals real interest rates!) are high, there is usually not much interest in gold. But when real interest rates are negative, gold prices can tick up owing to investors' fear about inflation or loss of purchasing power. Another example of correlation that relates to the dollar is confidence. When confidence wanes, usually the dollar isn't far behind. Strong confidence in America conversely usually translates into a strong dollar. Now just to throw a fly in the economic soup, we'll give you (Forgive us our trespasses!) the formal definition of correlation. We just knew you couldn't wait.

CORRELATION is a statistical measure of the relationship, if any, between a series of numbers representing data of any kind.

To put that in laymen's language it simply means, as we already pointed out, some things prove to be related to other things; and, yes, some things proved not to be related to other things. When correlation is positive it is related; when correlation is negative it is unrelated. If you need a more, clear-cut definition of negative correlation, try divorce. If straw hats in winter and skis in July are presumably cheaper, then go out and buy flood insurance during a monsoon if you want to pay a premium because 9 of 10 times there will be a positive correlation. So there you have it. Correlation might lead you to think about hedging.

Hedging? How did that get in here? Well, not everything usually goes up all at once in your life, just as everything usually doesn't head south all at once either. You have a homeowner's policy on your home? That policy is a hedge some would call it a put option, against a fire or some other untoward accident that could damage the value of your house. Same thing holds true with earthquake or flood insurance if you happen to live in California. (Yes, the Golden State occasionally has a flood or two or an earth slide owing to a monsoon.) There is a negative correlation there; you just never thought about it that way before. The only way the policy can become more valuable is for something negative to happen that would make your house less valuable. If your house catches fire and sustains $50,000 of damage, you'll quickly appreciate just how valuable that policy becomes, notwithstanding that $1,000 premium you bitched about paying every year. So, correlation is important if for no other reason then it can start those big wheels of gray matter turning about ways to hedge in case that Big Rock Candy Mountain turns out to be a big pile of baking soda.

Leverage and **liquidity** is what the 2Ls stand for, and taking the second one first, as we have already briefly mentioned, liquidity is about there being a market when and if you need one. It is synonymous with circulation, and just as healthy organisms need circulation to remain healthy so do markets. A simple gas, for example, like oxygen has to have a way in and, though later converted to another gas, carbon dioxide, a way to get out. Well, liquidity is the oxygen of all markets. Some events, like certain people, are noted for sucking all the oxygen out of a situation. The Russian bond default in 1998 might come to mind. And Bill Clinton was noted for sucking all the oxygen out a room full of other dignitaries. In physiology it's called breathing. Buyers may want to get in and sellers may want to get out. As long as both are plentiful markets will have liquidity.

Our point here is these are things you need to think about; some just don't want to be troubled. And that's fine. At the risk of sounding once again repetitive, it is a semi-free nation; you can choose to burn up your brain cells just about anyway you want with the apparent exceptions now of puffing smoke, wolfing down double cheese burgers with an extra-large order of fries and quaffing super-size sugar-laden soft drinks. And while we're at it along those lines, a June/July 2004 article in "Men's Fitness" quoted a study pointing out that nearly three-quarters of folks following low-carb diets "aren't cutting enough carbs to significantly lose weight." The study went on to say that low carb-dieters are consuming an average of 128 grams of carbohydrates a day, nearly six times the amount most high protein diets suggest. And an article in the *Wall Street Journal* in June 2004 noted researchers were discovering that so-called low-carb diets were actually causing people to eat more, nullifying any advantages one might gain from a low-carb diet.

We also mentioned leverage in the chapter on equities and buying on margin. Leverage is the high protein diet of investing, to be used but used with caution. Getting your grubstake blown up because you're greedy and over-extended is dumb. Let's say that again, dumb. If that sounds too harsh, turn us in to the PC police. If you take out a second mortgage on your home to finance a vacation or a new pogo stick while you're still shouldering thousands of dollars of credit card debt with rates of 14 or 15 percent, that is dumb. If you buy a $6 stock on margin with money you got from the second you took out on your home because your aunt Minnie got a tip from the clerk at Costco about a firm that is about to market a product that will wipe out the need for paper toilet seat covers at airports everywhere without first doing some checking, that too is dumb. If you have all your nest egg tied up in your employer's stock, ala Enron, only three words can describe it: dumb, dumber and dumbest. Leverage is like the ocean or the sky, both wonderfully marvelous in their own way, but terribly unforgiving to those who fail to show the proper respect.

Now for the 3Vs, **velocity, volume** and **volatility**, velocity is about turnover, in this case the turnover of money. Why do you think the Fed lowers interest rates or makes credit easier to obtain, so you'll horde the green stuff? Spend is the term you're searching for; they want you to spend. It turns out that velocity increases when inflation shows up because if you live in a place like the U.S. you could be losing purchasing power by the month. If you live in a third world nation you could be losing it by the second. If you're losing it by the month it is called inflation, by the second hyper-inflation. Does hyper-inflation ever happen? Of course, just look at Germany after World War One or the monetary history of many Latin American countries.

Now velocity can slow down during recessions because folks get troubled about the prospect of losing their jobs, so they tend to hold on to what cash they have. Two-thirds of the $11 trillion or so U.S. economy is based on consumption. Imagine (We know it's difficult, but try anyway!) if U.S. consumers suddenly closed their purses. To folks like Alan Greenspan (Or Ben Benanke, remember him?) and politicians that's a scenario that could become more harsh than rap music. There is still another time when the velocity of money slows and in 2003 it was much on the lips of central bankers, falsely so in our opinion, but that's what makes for horse races, deflationary times. Whereas during inflationary periods money is getting weaker and weaker, worth less and less, during deflation money is like a bodybuilder loading up on steroids before a big event, getting stronger and stronger, becoming worth more and more.

Now here is a question: If your purchasing power, your dollar, is getting stronger and stronger everyday, why would you choose to purchase anything today or, for that matter, repay your debts? Contrast that with a buck that comes down with a bad case of anemia and is constantly getting weaker. You would probably, like in the 1970s, not wait to purchase an item because tomorrow it is only going to cost more. And why would you mind paying your creditor back with an asset that is depreciating steadily? You're actually in a state of slow motion default on your debt. Central bankers use this to monetize their way out of debt. In less polite circles it's called counterfeiting. Ever notice how seriously the Treasury Department and the IRS go after counterfeiters and tax dodgers. If you had a monopoly, what would you do to protect your turf? Child molesters, rapists and serial killers go to jail and often get paroled. When is the last time you heard anything about counterfeiters? You bought an item on credit that cost you a dollar; you're now repaying your creditor with an asset that will cost him or her, should they chose to buy the same item, a $1.24.

So pay attention to velocity and while you're at it check out volume and volatility. Volume usually has to do with interest as in attention-getting; usually the greater the interest, the greater the volume. Check out new home sales the past couple of years. And those tech wonders of the 1990s got lots of attention as evidenced by soaring volume. In the futures market (Yes, it is a subject we know we haven't brought up before.), traders talk about the number of open contracts. That has to do with volume. Every trading day market mavens discuss up volume and down volume, heavy volume and light volume. Just before holidays volume tends to be light as traders head out of Dodge early. Volume often times is light before important announcements. Volume can also be quite heavy before some piece of bad news hits the airways.

We have pretty much discussed the 2Ps, **politics** and **position**; and if you don't understand spread by now, well, you'll probably get caught up in a spread squeeze some time in your investing future, like owning a variable rate mortgage in a rising interest rate scenario. As for the spread you should note that the spread in mid-2004 between short-term Treasury bills and long-term T-bonds was near 70-year highs. That translates into a pretty steep yield curve (remember yield curves?). It also makes the carry trade possible. Now of course the spread could widen, but with interest rate hikes by the Fed in the offing, that spread is likely to narrow, maybe even go to an inverted yield curve if the Fed gets too aggressive. (In early January, 2006 the yield curve indeed did invert!)

And, oh by the way that third P, what does it stand for you want to know? It stands for **Premium**. And premium is to spread as spread is to risk if you get my drift. When things are more risky, more volatile, less predictable the premium attached to them is usually higher. Say you get half a dozen tickets, speeding or otherwise, in one year. Does your insurance premium go up assuming you can even get coverage? You bet, because you are viewed as more volatile, more risky. Are you less predictable? Well, that depends on how you look at it. Like most folks, insurance companies don't like uncertainty anymore than anyone else, including the stock market. By the way, the stock market is comprised of individuals, thousands of individuals. It's pretty hard to get more unpredictable than that.

CHAPTER FIFTEEN

Knowledge without wisdom is a load of books on the back of an ass.

Japanese proverb

UNCOMMON WISDOM

As ironic as it may sound, there is perhaps no place on earth where wisdom is as uncommon as Wall Street. With its clutch of over-compensated brain power and enough MBA degrees to gag even the most ardent academician, Wall Street for all its fabled history is the epitome of the fellow who, no matter what he does or how fortunate he is, just can't stand prosperity. You need to recognize this from the get-go because it is your prosperity, not theirs, they just can't stand. With the possible exception of degrees in education, MBAs are the most over-rated sheepskins in the history of academia. That's probably why they cost so much; anytime something becomes in demand, the price escalates, in many instances, so far as to exceed the value of the product. That Wall Street is loaded with more MBAs per capita than probably any other profession should set off the alarm bells for you.

So how do you as an ordinary investor navigate some of Wall Street's rocky shoals without washing ashore, poorer for your journey? First thing to learn is what we call The Guru Rule. Simply stated, the Guru Rule says there are NO gurus. Anyone who has been even vaguely associated with the stock market for any length of time will, if honest, acknowledge that he or she has been wrong more times than he or she would care to publicly admit. The key word here is publicly. Or if you're of a legal or journalistic bent, try on the record. That doesn't mean that, after doing some homework, you should never subscribe to various newsletters or magazines or journals or, alas! tune in even to some of those financial television or radio farces. The truth is you can learn a lot from those who pretend to know a lot. What the guru rule says is nobody, and we mean nobody, is correct all the time. In fact, few are even right most of the time. But you don't have to be correct all the time.

Another rule though it may sound a bit Zen-like has to do with life's lessons. People spend much money and time seeking to learn life's major lessons, queuing up sometimes for hours at famous retreats and watering holes. Since markets are composed of people, they are a reflection of life. And there is only one lesson. There is no lesson; everything is going to surprise and the only way to engage that surprise is to open up your self. Expect the unexpected. And don't think for a moment experience always begets wisdom. It doesn't. As former president John F. Kennedy noted after his Bay of Pigs Cuban fiasco: "How could I have been so far off base? All my life I've known better than to depend on the experts." And Wall Street probably has more so-called experts per square foot than even the nation's capitol. You might want to conjure thoughts of the Pentagon here.

It may be location, location, location when it comes to real estate, but when it comes to learning it is repetition, repetition, repetition. So at the risk of being a little repetitious, the key most experts claim opens the door to true learning, we'll repeat something we pointed out earlier. To make money you only have to be correct 51 percent of the time. If you are right, say, 56 or 60 percent of the time you'll need to back up old Peter Lynch's truck to cart off your winnings. Lynch in case you're not familiar was the money manger that put Fidelity's Magellan fund on investors' map before he decided to cash it all in; Lynch made a lot of money for a lot of people, including himself; he also made a lot of errors.

Funny thing about human nature, whenever we make a passel of money we tend to forget the losses, just as the reverse is also true. If for some twisted reason you think we're way off base with that 51 percent figure, remember this: they reward baseball players gargantuan bucks to hit a baseball safely 33 percent of the time. Check out the number of homeruns Barry Bonds hits versus his number of bats, notwithstanding how many times he is intentionally walked. Some baseball experts claim that if Bonds weren't walked intentionally so often, he would hit even more homeruns. Yes, and he would also increase his chances for striking out more and making more outs. Hitting a speeding 90 mile-plus an hour baseball consistently may be a tad harder than consistently making money in the market, but just a tad. And for that matter what is the percentage of completions for most high-paid NFL quarterbacks?

And that brings us to the second point, what should you do those other times when you discover you're wrong. The answer is a four-letter word: SELL. Yea, we know that it flies in the face of the human condition, but cutting your losses is every bit as important, maybe even more so because it is so difficult for most investors to do, as selecting winners. We don't know if your first loss is the best loss; we just know that hardly anyone can afford to take lots of big losses. Big wins, yes; big losses, no. To put it differently, you might say the more small losses you have, the fewer number of large wins you need to come out ahead. So that should set your incisive, cunning little mind asking not what can go right about an investment selection you have decided to make, but rather what can go wrong. Because if you figure out what can go wrong and recognize it when it happens, you'll be able to keep those losses small. On the other hand, if the things that can go wrong don't go wrong, you may have found yourself a winner. And we can hear the truck engine purring now.

You need to realize that much of the research Wall Street foists on the retail investing public is almost as flawed as CIA intelligence. You need to realize that there are many Street analysts like the former Henry Blodgett who publicly hype stocks they privately believe are POSs. (Aw, c'mon use your imagination here!). Wall Street denizens willing to sell their souls to a bubble should not surprise you. Accounting scandals, mutual fund hanky panky, insider trading, many would have you think that these are isolated incidents. Not so. In 1940 Fred Schwed Jr. wrote what is now a classic called *Where Are the Customers' Yachts? Or A Good*

Look At Wall Street. A former Wall Street broker himself during the Great Crash of 1929, Schwed recounts example after example that such transgressions have been around as long as the Street has been around.

So just how repetitive are things on Wall Street? Well, the answer is far too repetitive to give many details in a book (sorry, manual) this size, so we'll just cite a few. And there is no place better to start than at the top. In the 1930s after the stock market crashed, the chairman of the New York Stock Exchange went to jail for fraud. In early 2004 New York Attorney General Eliot Spitzer (is there anyone this guy hasn't sued?) brought charges against Richard Grasso, former NYSE chairman, not for fraud but for being overly compensated. Greed doesn't always have to be illegal.

In 1923 Edwin Lefevre's *Reminiscences of a Stock Operator*, a fictionalized biography of Jesse Livermore, was published. Livermore in real life was one of the most respected, flamboyant, colorful stock and commodity traders ever. He made fortunes, lost them and remade them. Just out of grammar school, Livermore started his career as a quotation-board boy, posting stock prices on the big board in what was then known as the customers' room. Here is a quote that in many ways summarizes Liverpool's years on Wall Street.

Another lesson I learned early is that there is nothing new in Wall Street. There can't be because speculation is as old as the hills. Whatever has happened in the stock market to-day has happened before and will happen again. I've never forgotten that. I suppose that I really manage to remember when and how it happened. The fact that I remember that way is my way of capitalizing experience.

It should be noted that many people over the years have described *Reminiscences of a Stock Operator* as the best book on the market they have ever read.

Between 1997 and 2000 a lot of so-called growth stocks got pushed at the public; most were part of the new-paradigm palaver. Much of the Wall Street babble at the time forecast many of these goodies were going to embarrass Jack's famous beanstalk on their way skyward. "My favorite definition of a growth stock," the late Burton Crane wrote in

The Sophisticated Investor, "is 'a stock somebody is trying to sell you.'"
A journalist for the *NY Times*, Crane covered Wall Street for many
years, and the above comment appears in Chapter 10 entitled: "If They
Say 'Growth' Make 'Em Prove It." His book first appeared in 1958
and between 1958 and 1963 went through 10 printings. So somebody
must have believed it had value. Crane further noted that in the early
1950s industries like chemicals, paper, distillers and frozen foods were
high on the growth-stock list, but by 1958 their "growth was barely
discernible to the naked eye."

A modern day example might be Intel, one of the chip darlings of the
1990s growth stock era. When the company reported its earnings for
the third quarter in early October 2004, the *Financial Times* noted:
"….it is worth recalling that annual revenue growth since 1997 now
looks set to amount to a miserly 4.2 percent at Intel, a supposed growth
stock. Much of its market has matured since then—unlike investors."
It should also be noted Intel's miserly prospects occurred when U.S.
after-tax corporate profits as a share of national income in 2004 were
at their highest level in more than 50 years, a feat that has happened
only four other times in history, suggesting that further gains from
such lofty heights would require lot of blood, sweat and luck. And by
the way, on those four other occasions corporate profits subsequently
returned to a significant level below trend. You should be thinking
regression to the mean!

The fact is in the last 75 years there have been not one but three so-
called "new eras." The first in the 1920s, the second 40 years later when
one-size-fits-all growth stocks, commonly referred to at the time as the
Nifty Fifty, became the rage and the third and probably the biggest
in the 1990s. And all three shared several common characteristics; a
belief that the ordinary business cycle was DOA; low-to-moderate
inflation coupled with a strong economy; and a seemingly undying but
unfounded faith in technology, government and equities. For the sake
of pounding the point home and for the historically-challenged, these
three so-called "new eras" were themselves not new.

Here is Livermore describing his early success. "We ran into the big
boom of 1901 and I made a great deal of money—that is, for a boy."
Livermore then recounts the tenor of the times. "The prosperity of the

country was unprecedented. We not only ran into an era of industrial consolidations and combinations of capital that beat anything we had up to that time, but the public went stock mad....we had a three-million share day. Everybody was making money.....A wonderful time! And there were some wonderful winnings. And no taxes to pay on stocks sales! And no day of reckoning in sight." To get some idea of what a three-million share day meant, Livermore recalls how he up to that time had only heard stories about previous economic booms where Wall Street denizens boasted fondly about 250,000 share days. Even for those who remained semi-comatose during the recent dot-com mania the similarities should be striking: prospects for unprecedented prosperity; capital gains taxes lower than that levied on ordinary income; huge amounts of capital freely floating about; an economic scenario far beyond what most up to that time had ever seen in their lives; enormous volume; a public gone equity crazy; and, supposedly, with all those new paradigm claims, no "day of reckoning in sight."

Throughout this chapter we have been talking about things that could be loosely described as investing techniques. We say loosely because anytime you write something in stone you're apt to be disappointed. Putting things in concrete should remind you of all those exam questions in school with "always," "never," and "forever" in them. Good exam takers spot them right away. You should also recall the line in the Greek tragedy, *Antigone*: "The inflexible heart breaks first."

So how about some tips from an unlikely source? Alan Goehring is a 41-year old former New York bond trader. Goehring took Horace Mann's advice literally and, still in his 20s, went west to seek his fortune. While romping around the Southern California beaches he learned to play Texas Hold'em, a variation of poker where no-limit betting is allowed. In 2003 Gohering won the World Poker Tour Championship, the Super Bowl of poker and along with it the $1 million-plus pot. But that was hardly his first big win. In 1999 he raked in another rainbow worth more than $700,000. Here are some of the things Gohering learned over the years.

1. Follow your joy or as the poetic might put it, follow your own muse. Find out what makes you happy and do it.

2. Learn by doing. You're not going to improve your investing results via osmosis. You have to get in there and crack a few eggs. Ask questions, read manuals (er, books). Toss in some newspapers and magazines and a healthy dose of skepticism while you're at it.

3. Don't be a follower. Gohering talks about how trying to emulate others caused him to lose more than he won until he returned to being himself. There is probably only one Elvis, one Frank Sinatra, one Michael Jordan, one Ray Charles and one Warren Buffett. How many rich Elvis impersonators do you know? In other words, play your own game, develop your own style. In the early 1950s there was a young acting phenomenon named James Dean and his slightly older contemporary, the incomparable Marlon Brando. Over the following decades thousands of actors tired to emulate them, hoping to find their place in celluloid stardom, but all these years later there is still only one Dean and one Brando. And ditto Elvis.

4. Have fun. To be a great player he recommends not taking it all too seriously. This sounds like good advice for life, too. Wanting to win and having as much fun as possible along the way are hardly mutually exclusive.

5. There are no easy answers. This is another take on the no-free lunches theme. Gohering says poker is neither physics nor science. You can have two experts play the same hand differently. (Sounds like most courtroom trials! Anyone thinking O.J. Simpson here?) He relates how to get to the championship round he played hands that 80 percent of the experts would never play. So it's not written on high how to be successful despite what many would have you believe.

6. It is how you play the game. This is another way of saying it's not what stakes, small or large, you start with, but how you use what you already have. And we all have something.

Now just for the record if you find taking advice from a card player troubling, remember this: Bill Gross the Pimco bond guru experienced more than a modicum of success in Las Vegas as a card-counting black jack player in his previous incarnation.

CHAPTER SIXTEEN

Let be be the finale of seem. The only emperor is the emperor of ice cream.

Wallace Stevens

REALITY

Everyone has opinions. And that's really all they are, opinions. Not to get religious here, but religion teaches all are imperfect. Woman (man) is flecked and flawed, opinionated. Now we could pull a real switch and say flecked and flawed, imperfect and opinionated are synonymous with illogical and irrational. For several years we used to teach a class at night and we'd always start every first session with the same question.

"If you saw any irrational behavior today, please raise your hand?"

Not a single hand would go up. Then we would ask our second question.

"If you drove your car to school tonight, raise your hand?"

This was Southern California, God's gift to concrete, automobile manufacturers and carbon dioxide. Several years earlier, before diamond lanes and commuter parking lots, as an undergraduate one of our professors came bounding into class one warm spring afternoon excited, almost breathless; and when a student asked what was up, he told the class he just got off the Freeway where he actually saw a car with two people in it.

Every single hand every single time would go up in response to our second question. Then we would repeat our initial question.

"If you saw any irrational behavior today, raise your hand?"

Think mad scientists here sequestered deep in their research cellars probing for the perfect formula for irrationality: three or four thousand pound metal and plastic objects with steering wheels attached with human beings behind them.

So here's a leap and it has nothing to do with faith. Markets are composed of women and men, people. If A + B = C is logical, and it is, then C – B must = A. But a funny thing happens when we give them names like Alfred, Betty and Charley. Alfred plus Betty is never going to equal Charley. And Catherine minus Bill is never going to equal Alonzo. So if markets are comprised of flecked, flawed, illogical, irrational, imperfect, opinionated people, whose is the fool here? We expect markets after we finish sizing them up or sizing them down to behave rationally, logically. As conventional thinking goes, illogic is the preserve of only the perverse. But here logic is a lot like astrology; it will mostly guarantee you the wrong answers. Would have, should have, could have, ought to, was supposed to, assumed to be, might of, hope to be, so-in-so said it would or said it was are all irrelevant.

If you think were exaggerating here, get a copy of Emanul Derman's, *My Life As A Quant*, (Wiley, 2004*), the subtitle of which *is Reflections on physics and finance.* As a young man Derman migrated from South Africa to the United States in 1966 to pursue his life's love, pure physics. After obtaining his doctorate at Columbia University, Derman drifted into applied physics, working at several famous research centers such as AT&T's Bell Laboratories before winding up as a trader at Goldman Sachs in 1985. At Goldman he was charged with developing an option pricing strategy for bonds. The oil shock of the early 1980s, still fresh in peoples' minds, had caused long gasoline lines for Americans, creating lots of market volatility particularly in the bond market; and in the minds of many volatility rhymes with villain. Financial modeling, not unlike its social counterparts, is supposed to offer a way to take the human element out of the equation. For many modeling, econometric or otherwise, has become the modern day version alchemy.

Let be be the finale of seem. The only emperor is the emperor of ice cream.

What that means to you and me is the only thing important when it comes to markets is what is-- not what might have been or should have been or could have been. We all may look through the looking glass, but we're all humans and humans never see things clearly completely. What it means is: What's the trend? Trends can of course change, but until they do that is what the market is. The above quote comes from perhaps Stevens' most famous poem, "The Emperor of Ice Cream" written in 1922.

Born in Reading, Pennsylvania, Stevens mimicked his father by going into the practice of law after attending Harvard and New York University Law School. Following graduation and after a brief stint as a journalist he practiced law successfully in New York for a few years, writing poetry in his spare time, before moving to Connecticut where in 1916 he took a position with what then was called the Hartford Accident and Indemnity Company. In 1923 he published his first volume of poems and at age 44 became known as one of the "new" younger poets. By 1934 he was a vice president at Hartford. A man of business and worldly affairs, Stevens' poetry gained a reputation for its difficulty, hardly given to the easy quote, choosing to follow the poetic rather than the rationally logical, not given to any quick understanding that earmarked most popular poetry at the time.

As humans we tend to look at things in contrast. Vanilla versus chocolate, green beside pink, this is good compared to that and so forth. Don't forget in English we still have the comparative case, fat, fatter and fattest, something the PC crowd is doing everything in their warped earnestness to eradicate. We only think we see things in their totality. We only think we know, to quote Paul Harvey, "the rest of the story." If the decision to invade Iraq comes to mind here, you're starting to remove your light from under that peach basket.

We never know what someone else thinks about us just as we almost never tell someone how we really view him or her. A client who for years ran a very successful business was for years after his office manager to tell him what she really thought of his management style. One day while sitting in her office, following much cajoling on his part, she finally did. He sat there in silence, noting it all. When she concluded, he quietly got up, walked to her office door, turned and said: "Remind me to tell you what I think of you someday." Stevens' poetry is about ideas that seek to illuminate rather than run from reality. The reality of the market is: what is it doing now and what should we as investors make of it? In other words, forget about what you should do and start focusing on what you really do. While writing this manual for six months I was going to better organize my office. Six months later I was still looking for some graph or chart I had laid somewhere to include in the manual. That's a characteristic of human nature; that all humans don't succumb to it doesn't change the characteristic. If we've said this once, it bears repeating: markets are comprised of humans. In truth, that fact is most likely markets' biggest flaw. Locate human beings and you'll find irrationality and even chaos, a fact of life that the poor, little minds of the PC crowd just can't comprehend. But if you seek to make money investing, you better comprehend it and the sooner the better.

As two of the more insightful philosophers of their time, Gilbert and Sullivan noted: "Things are not always what they seem. Skim milk masquerading as cream." Early in my career I was working in the Emergency Room and one night around three in the morning they rolled in a respectable-looking little elderly lady complaining of chest pain. The way she was decked out you didn't know if she had been to a wake or a wedding. She had on a black hat with a veil; brand new long sleeved black dress with black shoes, a black pair of those mid-calf hose and the requisite rogue and lipstick. A white sales tag still dangled from the back of her dress.

One of the ambulance attendants volunteered that when he and his partner got to her home, she made them wait a good 10 minutes while she was getting ready. When the nurses began to strip her down to start an IV and hook up the EKG monitor, however, they discovered from just above her clavicles to the top of those mid-calf hoses one big, continuous sheet of dirt. The stuff was caked on in thick, hard layers like baked enamel. An intern who claimed he grew up on a Midwest farm later joked that she had enough dirt packed on that tiny 100-pound frame to grow a couple of acres of soybeans. She wound up in CCU with an MI, and it took three nurses two days and four complete baths to finally scrub off all that topsoil.

And it isn't about brains either. Brains more often than not are about logic. The S&P 500 between 1984 and 2000 regularly coughed up 16.3 percent returns. Over the same 15-year period the Mensa Investment Club, an organization that symbolizes, hope no one tells the ACLU, the quintessence of discrimination since it accepts only the smartest of the smart, managed an annual return of 2.5 percent. And how do you explain all those high-priced soothsayers, economic and otherwise, who so frequently turn out to be wrong?

In 1998 William A. Sherder's The *Fortune Sellers: The Big Business of Buying and Selling Predictions* landed in books stores. A business consultant, Sherder spent years tracking the predictive accuracy of several important areas that impact our lives, meteorology, economics, investments, technology assessment and futurology, to name a few. Forecasting and consulting is a $10 billion a year business. But just how accurate are their forecasts? Not too, Sherder documents. Meteorology has a scientific basis, he notes, but even it is hardly reliable. As a kid growing up in a small town we lived a good 150 miles from a big city where the U.S. Weather Bureau had its official forecaster. Time after time the local guy proved to be more correct than the big city bureaucrat. It became somewhat of a regional joke until one day a radio station called up the local guy to find out how he did it. "Well, it isn't too difficult," the local forecaster jovially offered, "I just find out first what they're saying at the U.S. bureau and predict the opposite."

And here is one more piece of evidence. Academic studies have shown that the orange juice concentrate futures market is more accurate at predicting Florida weather patterns than meteorologists. And there is that presidential futures market at the University of Iowa in Iowa City. It is almost never wrong at predicting the eventual winner.

With economics the record is murkier still. Sherder cites a 1985 article by "Economist" magazine that compared the accuracy of UK sanitation workers' predictions with the heads of several top-drawer multinational economic firms about England's future economic growth. The results: they tied. And analyzing data from 1975 to 1995 about economic forecasts predicting major turning points in the U.S. economy, Sherder relates 46 of the 48 he tracked were incorrect.

To put some further bite in the Sherder's data bark, in July, 1982, with the prime rate at 16 ½ percent the *Wall Street Journal* surveyed leading economists about their outlook for interest rates for the end of that year. Most claimed the prime rate would remain at 15 percent or end up even higher. Alan Greenspan, still toiling away on Wall Street, predicted rates would finish the year at 16 percent. Their take on the stock market was no less gloomy. By mid-October, however, the prime rate had been cut seven times and wound up 1982 at 11.5 percent. The dramatic rate-reversal pumped new juice into the stock market and the DJIA rallied 34 percent by yearend.

You don't hang around this business for nearly 25 years and fail to learn something. Earlier we quoted Jim Collins, author of the best selling *Good to Great* ......"Good is the enemy of great." Any good diagnostician can diagnose a common disease when it presents with common symptoms. A great diagnostician, however, diagnoses the same disease when it shows up dressed for the Mardi Gras. Stevens' poem is about choice, choosing the real over the apparent. As already noted, markets are about what is, about reality. Generation after generation too many of the retail masses go marching in tandem across the investment landscape only to be deceived by appearance. The parade looks good, there are lots of floats and confetti, marching musicians and long-legged majorettes and, as always, jumping on the bandwagon is the easy thing to do.

CHAPTER SEVENTEEN

It is not from the benevolence of the butcher, or the brewer, or the baker that we expect our dinner, but from their regard for their own interest.

Adam Smith

TAXES

It would be difficult if not remiss to write a manual about investing without including something about taxes and the Internal Revenue Service. Irrespective of your love of country or patriotic feelings, the IRS and its tax collectors are an impediment to your investing goals, assuming you have any. Fair is fair is an old bromide, but hardly anyone can agree on the true definition of fair. And never commit the mishaps of thinking that fairness has anything in common with simplicity.

If you subscribe to redistribution theory, then the progressive tax scheme currently being used is fair. On the other hand, if you believe everyone, notwithstanding his or her income level, should pony up at least some taxes, then the current system hardly meets the fairness doctrine. The progressive system is based on the assumption that those who have more should pay more and those who have less should pay less. No place therein is it stated that those who have more possibly work harder or longer to have more and those who have less do just the opposite. And no place therein is it stated that in a semi-free country such as the good ole USA that this is an individual choice. But like many things in life, it all sounds good in theory. The trouble is, as in Bill Clinton's definition of is, who gets to decide the meaning of more and who gets to decide the meaning of less. And likewise who gets to decide the meaning of progressive. For the better part of brevity, we'll leave most of that to the political pundits to fight out.

What you need to know is this: Whether you realize it or not, your freedom or leisure is directly related to your ability to finance it. Freedom is not guaranteed by the federal government or, for that matter, any other government. That's an erroneous assumption many in this nation hold to their own peril. Perhaps Christopher Morley said it best years ago: "There is only one success—to be able to spend your life in your own way." Now today's social crybabies would probably call Morley selfish. If that surprises you, you probably long ago deposited your head somewhere where the sun never shines. And that should be, in a semi-free nation like ours, your right. But for all the rest of us it's our right to follow Morley's dictate.

If you have one year of emergency or rainy day funds saved and you lose your job, you can take a little time to find another position. Contrast that to having no rainy day funds set aside. Resources are finite; isn't that one of the major arguments of the environmental crowd? The more money you pay in taxes every year, the less you have left to finance your leisure or freedom. But you don't have to lose your job to get the point. You could be in a two-income family, not all that uncommon today, when one person suddenly dies or just leaves, again not all that uncommon. And understand this point. Financial independence (and that's a definition that is different for nearly everyone), contrary to what some would promulgate, is not inherently immoral or evil or wrong anymore than being a person of color or belonging to a certain religious faith or choosing to paint your home pink or refusing to post your picture on one of those ubiquitous Internet dating sites is immoral or inherently incorrect.

Wealth is good. If you don't think so, then answer this question: Where would you rather live, in the wealthiest nation on earth, the U.S., or in some backwater third world country (less PC commentators have called them turd-world countries!) where the rule of law and property rights don't exist? If you opt for the latter, there is certainly nothing stopping you from moving there immediately. In this nation you still have that right, as long as you don't try to take too many of your possessions with you, like your bank account and you are not a corporation named Stanley Works. If you do you'll be labeled a traitor by the social do-good mob. Trouble is few folks in those backwater countries enjoy the same right. High standards of living are directly related to a nation's underlying wealth. If you think all the people, legal and illegal, flocking to America today are just seeking political asylum, you need to sign up for Economics 101. High taxes rob nations of their economic wealth. High taxes rob you of your ability to finance a self-sufficient life and retirement.

Here is a little arithmetic test. We're sure you can do the math. Back in 1913 when the Internal Revenue Service became more than just a gleam in some greedy politician's bifocals, the tax code was barely more than 100 pages. That was then, this is now. The *Standard Federal Tax Reporter* today, and this is no misprint, is a whopping 54,846 page, 25-volume gargantuan that would choke even the fattest, triple-chin bureaucrat twice. That's a 14,000 percent growth rate that makes the expansion over the years of the nation's GDP and the Dow Jones Industrial Average puny by comparison. But for the record here is a comparison. Between 1982 and 2000, an 18-year run that many believe culminated in the greatest bull market of all time, the DJIA rallied 1,409 percent. As previously noted, one of the popular management books making the rounds in 2004 contained this thought: "Good is the enemy of great!" If it takes 54,846 pages to create so-called fairness, you now know why fairness is the enemy of simplicity.

To put the growth of this gargantuan 54,846-page abortion into prospective, consider this: A little over 140 years ago Abraham Lincoln delivered his famous Gettysburg address. Recognized nearly universally now as a tour de force that defined the character of the American nation, Lincoln used a grand total of 268 words. The Declaration of Independence contains all of 1,300 words. Whether you are religious or otherwise, believer or non-believer, for or against school prayer, it took centuries to put the holy bible together. How many words does it have? Try 773,000. Compare that with our illustrious tax code's 9 million words, not to mention the 14,000 revisions to the code since just 1986.

And by the way, for those of you who support separation of church and state, protesting any displays or mention of God in public places, here's one for you: Why are we as a nation nearly everyday of the year swearing in witnesses and judges and justices at the highest level with one hand held skyward and other firmly fixed on the holy bible? They don't hold their right hands up and fix their left to the Koran or some other religious work. You'll need to figure that out for yourself.

While you're doing it you need to learn two things about taxes. There is evasion and avoidance; only one is illegal. Despite what the social engineers and social do-gooders spout, and for some reason we have a strong suspicion that they often fail to practice what they preach, like using birth control, taking advantage of so-called loopholes is neither immoral nor illegal. You need to learn that the government of itself has nothing; that the only way the government can give something to someone is to take something from someone else. So subsidizing prescription drugs or housing, for example, is done with money the government has taken from taxpayers like you and me. Or supporting boondoggles like ethanol with taxpayer money under the guise it's an energy- independence program rather than a handout to farmers. That you may not see such actions as either disturbing or troubling doesn't alter the facts. The only thing this government or any government in history has is what it extracts from others; and those extractions are hardly voluntary. In olden times those others were called subjects; today they are referred to as citizens. If you need *Webster's* to understand the difference, we suggest you look up euphemism while you're at it.

Back before Elvis Pressley finally left the building (We realize that many of you are too young to remember!), the federal income tax rate was 90 percent; that's right, old EP paid ninety cents of taxes on every dollar he earned. Over the years there have been numerous studies showing that when the federal income tax rate exceeds 25 percent, people begin to alter their behavior. That shouldn't surprise you. Check out an amoeba under a microscope in the lab. Even a primitive, unicellular animal changes or alters it direction whenever it encounters painful stimuli. Why should humans with a complex neurological system and a thumb, giving them opposition, be any different? And if you have not been paying attention to the importance of thumbs and opposition in the so-called progress of humankind, you just have not been paying attention. One of the hallmarks of left-wing liberals in this country is pointing out that there is more to patriotism than flag waving and paying your taxes. According to them, pointing out fallacies and faults with the system can also be patriotic.

And how correct they are. Nor is this to suggest that those on the right are any better: Same actors, different costumes. Tax and spend versus borrow and spend, the destination is the same. So if you'd like to keep more of your hard-won earnings, you might want to contact your Congressperson and urge the abolishment of the progressive tax system. It would be a patriotic gesture of the first order. The only fair tax would be a consumption tax; you use it, you pay it. Isn't that what Congress tried to do to smokers?

To protect yourself you don't need a six-shooter, pepper spray or a pit bull chained up in the back yard, though they might help. You need to be informed. Despite all their talk about education and its importance, an informed public is something bureaucrats and politicians and much of the media loathe. After all, what would a truly informed public need any of them for? (It was just a question, mostly rhetorical.) If you suggest you're too busy to keep informed, some would argue that you deserve what you most likely will reap—higher taxes and less leisure time and discretionary income. Just the opposite of what Morley was talking about.

Understanding taxes comes first with the question of whether you live in a high tax state. (As if all are not high tax states to their residents, you may be wondering. Actually, some states—Texas, Florida, Wyoming and Nevada, to name a few—levy no income taxes.) High state income taxes can easily push you into a much higher tax bracket, even though for now state taxes are deductible from your federal tax returns in most states. We say for now because none if this is written in granite.

Shell games have many versions. In prior years one had to worry about "bracket creep." As one's income rose it was not uncommon to wake up and discover one fine tax day that one was in a higher tax bracket. Well, for the most part bracket creep has been replaced by something many taxpayers are unfamiliar with, at least for now, something far more subtle and debilitating. It's called AMT, alternative minimum tax. We mentioned it briefly before. It's been around since 1970 when only 19,000 taxpayers felt its sting. In 2001 more than 1.4 million taxpayers experienced its bite. By most credible estimates that number by 2010 will jump to 36 million. If you don't know about it, you need to find out. It's not indexed to inflation, even the phony CPI-gauged kind. Your illustrious elected officials will claim it was just a slight over site and unless you start screaming now--long and loud and often-- they'll be telling you the same thing 10 years hence.

The United States is the world's largest debtor nation. Promoting consumption and taxing savings and investments is akin to letting a two-old go un-attended at the family swimming pool. You're embracing disaster.

If no manual on investing would be complete without a section on taxes, it goes without saying that in today's modern world no investing manual worthy of consideration would fail to mention information technology or IT and the Internet. If you were to sit down and try to devise one thing that would come closest to reflecting the world at large, it would probably be the Internet. It's all there: abstract and abstruse, bland and bizarre, bad and better, funny and foolish, excessive and exacting, healthy and hateful, hope and hype, lawless and legal, mediocre and majestic, new and old, passion and pornography, revolutionary and revolting, scholarly and slovenly, religious and secular, science fiction and scientific, you name it.

If you look up oxymoron in *Webster's* you'll find objective journalist. No such animal exists. One reason, as difficult as it may be to fathom, is journalists are members of the human species. And objectivity is yet to be identified anywhere in the human genetic code. Journalists and judges for the most part are about the only ones who get away with not declaring their party affiliations before they make their pronouncements. Imagine just how free the people in the Land of the Free would really be if judges, for example, were required to come into court everyday with a big sign on their chest that read: Democrat, Republican, Libertarian, sectarian, vegetarian, Presbyterian, Rotarian, socialist, nihilist, neo-con, ex-con, Catholic, protestant, Jew, Hindu, Muslim, agnostic, atheist, cyclist, pro-life, pro-death, pro-business, pro-labor, homosexual, asexual, heterosexual, undecided. And the only time you'll ever see objective journalists is when all the journalists are robots, and even then the robots will reflect the biases of those who programmed them, as in editors and publishers, which pretty much summarizes what we have today in the media. Programmers come in all forms from editors to professors.

The medium may be, as Marhsall McCluen indicated, "the message." But the media is about bias, make no mistake. And such biases are neither new nor novel. The list of journalistic dishonesty is long and lush. *USA Today* in 2004 finally fired a reporter for what turned out to be years of filing false stories. The fabled left-wing *New York Times*, noted for printing all the news fit to print, apparently doesn't mind printing some news of the unfit variety. The paper recently had a minority reporter who for months made up stories, yet higher-ups, though fully aware of it, were afraid to discharge him because of his race. The *Los Angeles Times* changed the content of a columnist's column whose political views they differed with, only later being forced to admit the charge was true. The *Boston Globe* in early 2004 apologized for running Iraqi war photographs that had not been authenticated before they were published are just a few examples. And then one of the more famous pre-election stories of the presidential election of 2004 involved CBS evening news anchorman Dan Rather and what turned out to be bogus documents questioning President George W. Bush's National Guard service in Texas during the Vietnam era. These are some of the largest media conglomerates in the world; many of them own not just print media but television and Internet services.

Despite the recent publication of former CBS producer Mary Mapes' book, "Truth and Duty: the Press, the President, and the Privilege of Power. (Now there is a presumptive title for you!), Miss Mapes' liberal leaning activism dates back to her earlier journalistic days in Seattle. For those who argue that leopards can change their spots, then explain all those liberals at the confirmation hearings for Supreme Court Justices seeking to persecute and block based on the candidates past. Liberals and leopards like other political ideologues seldom change their orientations.

During the top of the bull market it was not uncommon to turn on MSNBC Bubble Vision daily and hear some stock market guru say that such and such a stock was a buy at any price. Many of these stocks at the time were trading at price to earnings ratios that discounted the Second Coming. In fact, it was not until after the market blew up that MSNBC reporters started asking, no doubt at the behest of the network's legal department, their guest gurus if they owned or had any affiliation with the equities they were touting.

A constant caterwauling of the mainstream media about the Internet centers on reliability, credible information. The terms blog and bloggers have worked their way into the American lexicon. According to the entrenched, the new kid on the block, the Internet, offers certain dangers owing to the reliability of the sources and the credibility of the information one can get there. Anyone with an opinion can start a blog site or be a blogger. And that of course is true. But is the information supplied by the mainstream media any better? That's a decision you'll have to make for yourself. When you think of the mainstream media think of monopoly, think of those moat-surrounded companies Warren Buffet likes to gobble up. Think of anti-competition. Think of Bill Gates.

Those much-hated corporations, so despised by big media outlets like the *LA and NY Times* are at least vaguely responsible to shareholders and regulators. (And now maybe even Elliot Spitzer. How did he get in here? Let me hear someone say: "Greed! Ego! as in publicity.). The media is accountable to no one except your healthy dose of skepticism. And it's a dose of skepticism that you'd be well advised to continually cultivate. To paraphrase how one media writer recently put it, the public mandates that the media should be objective, transparent and balanced. We've already discussed objectivity and the media. Quoting un-named sources and stringing together so-called quotes from the gray matter of uppity-ups as if they were factual or the reporter was a mind reader hardly smacks of transparency. Quoting sources who request to go un-named is another classic example. Or attributing information to a "source close to the blah, blah" is another. And balanced is an accounting term with which, to paraphrase Einstein, the media has little truck because it comes from a world with which the media has absolutely nothing in common. Further evidence of the media's colored recklessness surfaces from time to time when retractions of once front-page stories wind up buried in the obit section. Only the aging and the affected regularly read the obit page.

How about an example you say. In late 2005 Congress in its infinite ability to do what Congress does best, waste taxpayer money holding hearings, held another one, this time calling in all the CEOs of the major oil companies to investigate charges of price gouging. At one point California Senator Barbara Boxer, a noted opponent of big business, dragged out a chart revealing the bonus CEO Lee Raymond of Exxon Mobile received the previous year. Though CEO remunerations were hardly the pretense for the hearings, the media ran with the story. It was quintessential Boxer, not to mention pure theater and a political ploy.

Four days later the *Financial Times* ran the following retraction in the sixth right hand column, half way down the page next to the center fold crease. One could find a classified ad selling aardvarks to Eskimos easier than finding this retraction.

"Lee Raymond, chief executive of Exxon Mobil, received $3.9m bonus in 2004, according to SEC filings, not $36m as wrongly reported in an article in some editions of the FT on November 10."

Incidentally, at the same time Congress was holding these hearings, carping about "obscene profits," Exxon earned 10 percent or 10 cents on the dollar. The same quarter Google, the Internet engine firm, was making 200 percent on the dollar. Obscene it turns out, like many other things in life, appears to be in the beholder's cash flow sheet.

The media routinely criticizes law enforcement for what is called "the blue code," a tendency for law enforcement officials to protect their own. The media blasts the medical profession, shouting for "physicians to heal thyself," condemning the profession's tendency to hang together against outside criticism and not weed out the medical malefactors. Ever present is the threat: If you don't clean up your act, we'll clean it up for you. Yet the very same media begins screaming like a bunch of scalded apes whenever anyone suggests holding their feet to the flame of outside accountability. In other words, only the elite media professionals, the anointed, are capable of self-regulation; the rest of society's poor slobs need outside over site. Only members of the media possess professional integrity. Surgeons operate unnecessarily; attorneys scam their clients; pharmaceutical companies plunder the public; dentists charge gold prices for amalgam fillings; preachers demagogue their congregations; accountants uncover but fail to report the Enrons and Global Crossings; Wall Street fleeces the unsuspecting and innocent. It's a great gig. The idea of a free, impartial media, since 1776 it is difficult to find a bigger hoax played on the American public. There is, however, a simple solution. Mandate that media members whenever they cover political events must sport nametags declaring their party affiliation and for whom they last voted. And like most other professionals, first time they are caught prevaricating, fine them. Second time, fine them more. Third time, ban them from the profession. If three strikes and you're out is good enough for hardcore criminals, it should be the perfect elixir for media members.

So journey, gingerly if you must, at your own peril down the road of so-called objective journalism, whether it is political, financial or otherwise. If you learn anything from this book (sorry, manual), we hope you now know that two of the major institutions in this society—institutions that can have catastrophic impact on your life and the quality of that life, the Federal Reserve Bank and the media—are absolutely accountable to no one.

EPILOGUE

There's not much in this old world worth one thin dime except old dogs, children and watermelon wine.

Country singer Tom T. Hall

A few years ago on a rather overcast Saturday morning while rummaging through one of those ubiquitous yard sales, I stumbled across a tattered copy of *Winning Strategies in Selling* by a guy named Jack Kinder. I didn't know then nor do I know now who Kinder was or is. Nor does it really matter. Just as I was about to toss the book back on a rickety old table something in the dedication caught my attention. It caught my attention not so much because it is about selling but rather because it is about what we have been trying to say throughout this manual. It's not about us; it's about you, your life, your future and your financial security. "Winners make things happen. Losers let things happen." To that we would add: Winners get informed, losers get upset. And you have to decide which one you're going to be.

Leafing through the pages I found my eye pulled to a simple graph reprinted below by permission.

If you earn:	Every hour is worth:	Each minute is worth:	In a year one hour a day is worth:
$25,000	$12.81	21¢	$3,125
$40,000	$20.49	34¢	$5,000
$50,000	$25.61	43¢	$6,250
$75,000	$38.42	64¢	$9,375
$100,000	$51.23	85¢	$12,500

Chart used with permission from Jack Kinder Jr. "Winning Strategies in Selling"

The above chart was published in 1981 and is not inflation adjusted.

In investing, like politics, the old saw about not being able to see the forest for the aspens holds true. Too many beginning investors focus on whom they get the information from rather than the quality of the information itself. To put it in a medical light, if you had a loved one incurably sick with cancer and you suddenly discovered that someone, in say, San Francisco, recall it's a pretty freaky town, for $20,000 truly had the cure, a cure that had been scientifically verified, how long do you think it would take to raise the money and book a flight? And when you arrived there and picked up the medicine, how much would you care if that person was homely, Hispanic, black, white, a pink puffer or blue bloater with a bad case alopecia, a walking triple-double-portion of French fries and Ben and Jerry's, octoroon or octogenarian? (And by the way, what's up with the PC Ben and Jerry; ninety percent of their product is pure fat! Where are the class action barristers when all those future diabetics need 'em)? The point is if you're really a truth-seeker you don't much give big plate of Spaghetti Carbonara where or from whom you get it.

I have always had a fondness for worn and tattered books. So with all due respect to Tom T. Hall, old dogs, children and the brewers of watermelon wine, I would add old books to that list and conclude with this: On your journey to financial-freedom or a sound retirement or just whatever your dream may be: Don't waste time or focus; they're all you really have.

We realize that some may criticize this manual for possibly being beyond the beginning- level investor. And we certainly considered that. Yet our intention was to write something informative, entertaining and thought-provoking though at times the idea of actually writing something thought-provoking seemed as foreign to us as humility is to most politicos, right or left. As we noted earlier we have always subscribed to the sink-or-swim approach, something much of the PC crowd views with askance if not downright contempt. That not everyone responds to this approach goes without saying. In a society that claims it loves to worship at the shrine of multi-pluralism, however, it should also go without saying that because not everyone responds doesn't justify banning the approach, something the PC crowd seems to get an air bubble in their Circle of Willis over and calls for every time anyone praises the sink-or-swim technique.

You the reader will decide if we've accomplished our goal. So we will leave you with this thought. While driving through south Alabama several years ago we came upon a restaurant that had a big sign out front. The sign said: "Great prices, great food, great service......pick any two."

And by the way one more important thing. Why a manual for nurses? According to the Labor Department there is currently a shortage in this nation of 100,000 nurses, a number the Department projects will jump to 800,000 by 2020.

So happy nursing and happy investing!

INDEX

X

Y

ABOUT THE AUTHOR

Ron Ellison, MA, is president of RLE & Associates, an independent research firm. He is founder and editor of the RLE GLOBAL REPORT, a no-nonsense review of world financial and geopolitical markets. A former journalist, Mr. Ellison has been following and investing in markets since the 1970s. He has been interviewed on radio and his writings have appeared in a variety of financial publications. Currently at work on a book about the great bull market that died in 2000, he is a registered investment advisor and a founding member of Blasingham and Ellison Financial Group, a private Newport Beach, California money management firm. He has taught courses in financial planning and is a frequent speaker on investment topics.

Nancy A. Downey, RN, MSN, NP has been a certified nurse practitioner for more than 20 years. Her medical experience is extensive, having worked in the private and public sectors in a variety of specialties ranging from geriatrics to general medicine, from lipid research to neurosurgery and urology. She currently heads up the liver transplant, Hepatitis C liver care program at the Long Beach Veterans Medical Center where her administrative duties include supervising 18 Nurse Practitioners and 4 Physician Assistants. Ms Downey is also a long-standing member of the Institutional Review Board at the medical center.

She is an instructor at the University of Phoenix in the undergraduate and graduate nursing programs where she is Area Chair for the Nurse Practitioner Program for the Southern California Campus. She is also an adjunct instructor at University of California, Irvine and a lecturer at California State University, Long Beach nursing programs. Ms Downey has published numerous abstracts and made numerous presentations to various professional and research conferences.

She resides in Long Beach, is an avid runner and an even more avid investor.

www.rleglobalreport.com

(877) 455-9681

Printed in the United States
79466LV00004B/280-327